PUNCHING

OUT

PUNCHING

....

OUT

Launching a Post-Military Career

FRED MASTIN

with

JOHN GRIDER MILLER

ST. MARTIN'S PRESS .... *New York*

Editor: Jared Kieling
Production Editor: David Stanford Burr
Copyeditor: Edward P. Paige
Designer: Sara Stemen

Library of Congress Cataloging-in-Publication Data

Mastin, Fred.
    Punching out : launching a post-military career / Fred Mastin with John Grider Miller.
        p.   cm.
    ISBN 0-312-10527-4
    1. Job hunting—United States.   2. Retired military personnel—Employment—United States.   3. Veterans—Employment—United States.
I. Miller, John Grider.   II. Title.
HF5382.75.U6M367   1994
650.14'024355—dc20   93-42661
                                    CIP

First Edition: March 1994

10 9 8 7 6 5 4 3 2 1

Books are available in quantity for promotional or premium use. Write to Director of Special Sales, St. Martin's Press, 175 Fifth Avenue, New York, New York 10010, for information on discounts and terms, or call toll-free (800) 221–7945. In New York, call (212) 674–5151 (ext. 645).

CONTENTS

Acknowledgments   ix

Introduction   1

Chapter One   THE TURNAROUND   5
*Facing involuntary retirement or release from
active duty • Winning through honest self-evaluation, clear goal setting, and methodical job
searching—a case study.*

Chapter Two   TAKING STOCK   20
*Regrouping around the six key areas of life • Taking
the essential self-inventory of experience, accomplishments, and skills.*

Chapter Three   MAKING CHOICES AND
                   SETTING PRIORITIES   35
*How to focus on your interests, needs, and dreams
• Setting your priorities among compensation, ca-
reer goals, and family needs.*

Chapter Four   WHAT'S REALLY OUT THERE—
AND HOW TO FIND IT   53
Recent trends in the job market • The new emphasis on quality and ethics • The first steps in your career search • A (not so) new way to discover career opportunities.

Chapter Five   THE RÉSUMÉ: A FOOT IN THE
DOOR   74
Capturing the high-speed early readers • Traps you must avoid • How to build the three basic résumés • How to write the all-important cover letter.

Chapter Six   GETTING THE INTERVIEW: HOW
TO OPEN THE DOOR   96
Two basic attitudes for the job search • Keeping a record—a must • Exploring the main routes to employment • How to start networking • Uncommon ways to land your job offer.

Chapter Seven   PREPARING FOR THE
INTERVIEW   114
How to maintain your perfect "ten" • Grooming for the workplace • The importance of bearing, voice, and mannerisms • Minding your manners • How to build the right wardrobe.

Chapter Eight   THE INTERVIEW   131
How the game is played • Screening, serial, group, and stress interviews • The fifteen ways you will be judged • The thirty-second barrier and the halo effect • Avoiding the tacky ten • How to handle the big questions.

Contents vii

Chapter Nine   NEGOTIATING THE JOB OFFER   156
Questions you *need to ask • Approaching the fol-low-up interview • How to tell when you are losing it • Why you should not take no for an answer • How to negotiate your salary and benefits package.*

Chapter Ten   LOOKING BACK . . . LOOKING
                   AHEAD   179
Listening for that one golden yes • Positioning your-self to move up in CivLand.

Resource Directory   181
Books, Periodicals, Organizations

About the Authors   186

Index   189

ACKNOWLEDGMENTS

Many wonderful people have helped bring this book into being—with a thought here, a bit of wisdom there. All their contributions have been valuable, but I must single out several individuals who played particularly significant roles.

The Honorable James E. Johnson, former Assistant Secretary of the Navy and a very dear friend, first pressed me to commit my experience in career transition to book form. Then he followed through, arranging contacts and providing constant encouragement as the project matured. I owe Dr. Johnson a great deal.

I also owe a lot to my friend and colleague F. James O'Neill, for his early assistance in pulling together the career-transition seminars that have produced many of this book's insights.

The rightful grandparents of this book are Joan Armstrong, Marlene Palmquest, and the staff of the Blackstone Memorial Library in Branford, Connecticut, who went far beyond the call of duty in helping me with research.

Nina Ryan of the Palmer & Dodge Agency in Boston found the right publisher and generally helped keep the project on track with strong professional advice and personal encouragement.

At St. Martin's Press, Senior Editor Jared Kieling and his assistant Ensley Eikenburg kept the draft manuscripts moving and provided much-needed cheerleading and insightful advice as the book neared its final form.

Without my collaborator, John Miller, this book would not have happened. His experience as author, editor, and career Marine was needed to pull everything together. John's wife Susan also deserves a great measure of credit—not only for her patient support but also for her ability to keep John's aging computer from crashing in midstream.

Very special thanks go to my dear wife Nancy, without whose strong support I could not have survived the turbulence of the past two years of book preparation.

A final tribute goes to the Georges and Susans I have worked with over the past twenty years, who have pulled things together to cross the bridge into CivLand. They have been my inspiration throughout, and I hope they will continue to inspire the readers of this book to follow in their footsteps.

PUNCHING

....

OUT

INTRODUCTION

S ometimes, a book can get started in a most improbable place. The seeds for this one were planted in March 1983, on board the amphibious command ship USS *Blue Ridge,* then—as now— flagship of the Seventh Fleet. We were ploughing through a late-winter storm, bound from Okinawa for the beach at Tok-sok-ri, Korea, where the amphibious portion of the annual Team Spirit combined air-sea-land exercise would take place. As a Marine Corps reservist on a thirty-day period of active duty, I was enjoying my sabbatical from my civilian job and getting to know some of the officers and noncommissioned officers from the Seventh Fleet and III Marine Amphibious Force staffs. Then the word got out: in real life, I was an executive recruiter—a "head hunter."

The sabbatical was over. During the day, the demands of preparing for the impending landing took over, but in the evening I became a career counselor, approached repeatedly by concerned Navy and Marine Corps officers. It was the most senior ones—the ones who had enjoyed the most success in their chosen military careers—who were the most anxious. They knew that this Far East tour of duty was probably their last, and that after one more "twilight" tour in the States they'd be facing mandatory retirement— at a time when they still had children in college and were paying off the biggest mortgages of their lives.

They knew they would have to find new careers, but they didn't know where to begin. And our unworldly isolation inside the steel hull as we bucked and heaved our way across the Western Pacific didn't help them much to get in the proper state of mind for a job search back in The World. They needed a bridge to civilian life, and for the moment I was it.

For me, that moment was only the beginning. Since 1983, I have crisscrossed the United States many times, talking and listening to men and women who wear the uniforms of all the armed services. I also have talked to countless employers, many of whom never saw military service, in a wide range of occupational fields. I wanted to find out how they perceive the strengths and weaknesses of military professionals as they reenter the civilian workplace.

I received two clear messages. The first should come as no surprise: The cold, cruel world is not misnamed. Things can be tough on the civilian side of the fence, especially in times of economic downturn. As the drawdown on the armed services continues, competition for civilian jobs will get even stiffer. Mental toughness always has been a prerequisite for playing the career game effectively; it will continue to be so.

The second message, on the other hand, should bring a new ray of hope.

THE COMMON THREAD

Several years ago, *The New York Times* published a study of the components of success. Researchers examined the backgrounds of thousands of Americans, from all walks of life, who had done reasonably well in their careers. The purpose was to discover what these successful people had in common.

The common denominator was not an affluent background—nor one of poverty. It was not ethnic heritage. There were no regional patterns, no geographical pockets of success anywhere in the nation. There were no schools with an inordinate percentage of successful graduates. Some schools did better than others, of course, but none stood alone.

When the analysis was complete, there was a single common thread: most of these successful people had served in the armed forces. Some were admirals; some were corporals. Some had served for more than thirty years; others did their five and took their dive. It didn't matter. The key was that most of them served.

It wasn't a matter of specific skills acquired in military service; the range of skills was nearly infinite. Rather, the common thread revealed itself in terms of shared personal traits:

> A high level of self-discipline
> A strong work ethic
> Willingness to accept responsibility and accountability
> Honesty and integrity, demonstrated in ethical conduct
> Physical fitness and appearance
> Forehandedness
> Practicality and attention to detail
> Innovation and creativity
> Extensive education and training
> Ability to make courageous decisions
> Steadiness under pressure; perseverance
> Dedication and loyalty
> Capability for motivational leadership

Your military service—whether for three years or thirty years—has helped you develop some or all of these traits that employers find so desirable. So you are off to a good start. But to pursue the career of choice, one that is driven by your interest rather than fear or economic necessity, some toil will be necessary. Opportunity often comes disguised as hard work, the saying goes.

In the past, you have been willing to make the extra effort needed to lower your golf score, improve your backhand in tennis, or knock several seconds off your distance runs. Is finding the career of your choice worth the same amount of sweat?

You will find blood, sweat, and even a few tears in this volume. Many people have contributed their hard-won experience to help make things easier for you. But take it slowly. We must approach the transition process step by step, and the first step is mental preparation. If you are looking for a shortcut, read no farther. You are not ready for what I have to offer.

But if you are willing to commit yourself to a dedicated search for a career that will get maximum mileage from your talents—a career you might even fall in love with—then stay with the program.

This program.

1
....

THE TURNAROUND

=====

T his is your captain speaking . . . "
    Uh, oh. The captain. First time he's been on the intercom since we took off from Los Angeles, and we're nearly to Chicago.

"We are in a holding pattern over Lake Michigan, about thirty miles east of O'Hare International. It's snowing, and they are stacked up a bit. I'll keep you posted."

No joy. I like Chicago, and even lived there for a while in the mid-1970s, but this time I just wanted to pass on through. I'd been out on the West Coast for two weeks, giving two five-day seminars on career transition. There were about thirty military folks in each, counting a few spouses, and we covered everything—even the way to negotiate a proper starting salary in a strange new civilian world. It was a total-immersion experience and it left me exhausted, but still emotionally high as I saw these men and women begin to look forward to a new phase in their lives, with new hope and new confidence.

"Folks—things don't look good in Chicago and neither does our fuel state. We may have to land in Indianapolis or Fort Wayne. I'll let you know."

There was a muffled outburst of unhappiness about two rows ahead of me. The gent had been flashing his tickets for that night's sold-out basketball game between the Chicago Bulls and the Detroit

Pistons. Tipoff was in two hours. Ah, yes—life is so unfair at times, and sometimes to just the right people.

I felt my own impatience begin to slip away as my thoughts went back to the seminars—then, after a while, to the best seminar ever. It was one of the first, nearly five years earlier, but it set the tone for all that followed. We convened at Camp Lejeune, the sprawling Marine Corps base on the North Carolina coast. The Marines and Navy were there, of course, but half of the twenty-eight attendees came from the Army's Fort Bragg, also in North Carolina, and Langley Air Force Base, in the Norfolk area. We had officers, staff noncommissioned officers, and their spouses. The group blended easily, quickly finding common interests, and after a while the members really began to care about each other. The common emotion that ran through the entire week was fear—fear of the unknown. Some of it was on the surface, but much more was deeply buried—and it had to be exhumed before we could begin to deal with it. By week's end, we had pulled out many of those deeper fears.

"Okay, folks—we've worked our way through the stack, and we are cleared to land at O'Hare. Flight attendants prepare for arrival."

So that guy's Bulls-Pistons tickets were still good, after all—that is, if the teams were still playing. I barely felt the wheels touch down. We were evermore in a blizzard.

Looking out from the passenger terminal, I saw that the snow plows were losing their battle in the streets. A handful of brave drivers gave it their best, but most of the cabs and buses were giving it up. I had seen enough. It was time to stake out a seat or a spot on the terminal's floor for the night.

But first I checked my address book, where I kept the phone numbers of old seminar members so I could check on their progress from time to time, especially during layovers.

There it was. George, from that great Camp Lejeune seminar, had headed for Chicago upon retirement. I soon had him on the line.

"Stay where you are. I'll be there in less than an hour," he said.

My thoughts drifted back to that Camp Lejeune seminar and my first encounter with George and his wife, Susan. That group turned out to be great, but the whole thing started on a bad note—and George was the problem. On the first day, he tried to tear into me, and when that didn't quite work he tore into his wife for luring him to the seminar, and brought her to the point of tears. I'd quickly had my fill of George, and so had the rest of the participants. I struggled to keep my cool until the first day ended. After class, I expected him to bug out, but he surprised me by hanging around until the others had left.

I was ready to strike first, but the words that came out took me by surprise.

"George, I'm glad you're here." (Did I really say that?)

"One of your friends spoke so highly of you that I've been looking forward to meeting you. I hope you can join me for lunch after class tomorrow." Clearly, George was thrown off balance.

The next morning, he wanted to apologize. We took it up at lunch, and the key to his explosive behavior began to surface. George was consumed by anger. He'd been tucking it away in his emotional cellar for the preceding two or three years, choosing not to deal with a number of unpleasant things that were intruding into his life. He would deal with them "later"—or perhaps they would just go away if he could ignore them long enough.

But reality had finally driven him to a decision point. George and Susan's youngest child, Sally, was afflicted with Down's syndrome, which required special counseling and schools. Such arrangements had to be made months in advance, but George—who had failed selection for promotion—now faced mandatory retirement from the Marines and had no idea of where he would be living or what he would be doing a few months from then. Frustrated, he had put off critical decisions—and now that frustration had boiled over into anger. George was mad at the Corps, his wife, himself, and the world in general. He had a relatively small pile of things to deal with, but he had let them grow into a mountain. Now, he was trapped on that mountain, with the fog rolling in.

George needed some healing. He seemed to be in a mild state of shock for the rest of the week. I couldn't tell just how much of the seminar he was absorbing. But the healing was taking place. I did not realize at the time how much the group was helping itself, comforting, encouraging, and giving some members a compassionate kick in the hindparts when the situation required.

THE BIG CHANGE

A wide guy in a red-and-blue ski jacket loomed in front of me and said, "Welcome to Chicago."

Was this the somber, shaky George I knew from Camp Lejeune? This George radiated joy and confidence, and had a neatly trimmed mustache, to boot. He gave me some foul-weather clothing and walked me out to his four-wheel drive jeep. We cleared the airport and moved onto Interstate 294, northbound. After passing the Glenview Naval Air Station, we turned off at Deerfield and finally pulled into the driveway of an attractive one-story brick home.

Susan greeted us at the door. She had to be in her midforties, but looked none of it. She and George directed me to a recliner chair in front of a radiant fireplace. It was a scene of supreme contentment, punctuated by the falling snow framed by the sliding glass doors of their family room.

What a change!

A few years earlier, their lives were in chaos. George was riddled by anger, fear, and a deep sense of failure. Susan was desperately trying to keep the family afloat, dealing with a number of problems their three children were experiencing. When I last saw them, they were rudderless, but just beginning to regain control. Obviously, they had done it.

"You both look terrific. I can't believe that you're the same people I saw five years ago."

"We aren't," said George.

Susan joined in. "When the group split up that Friday afternoon, we were numb—almost in a state of shock. We knew we had a lot of ground to cover, and less than seven months to get there.''

"How did you get started?"

"I needed time to sort things out," Susan said. "The weekend after your seminar was too busy, but on Monday morning—as soon as everybody left for work or school—I finally had some solo time. I took a long walk with my thoughts. When I got back, I started making two lists: 'What's Right' and 'What's Wrong' in my life. The first list didn't take very long. I could have written it on a postage stamp. But 'What's Wrong' took a full page and covered everything from George to my miserable tennis game. At the bottom of the list, I added SUSAN in big letters. I'd been passing out a lot of blame, and maybe some of it belonged to me.

THE FIRST STEP

"The first thing to deal with was George and me. We had been drifting apart, and our marriage was losing its direction and its intimacy—not sexual, but in closeness and sharing. We had always shared everything, the good and the bad. We were crushed when we learned that Sally would never live a normal life, but dealing with that together gave each of us added strength. Sometimes pressure can do that. Yet somehow our special relationship was breaking down. We were losing it.

"If we were ever going to get our act together, the time had arrived. I called a close friend and told her it was do-or-die time. She was great about it, and agreed to take the kids for the evening. I did some shopping, and fixed George's favorite dinner before I fixed myself up for a special evening. I wanted to dazzle him.''

"It was great," George said. "Later on, we called it our 'summit meeting.' Susan just looked me in the eye and said, 'I love you, George—and I want to be your best friend again.' We had to open some doors that had been locked for several years.

"It didn't take us long to get to the basic problem. It all started when I was passed over for promotion to lieutenant colonel. I was totally taken by surprise—ambushed! Up to that point, I had always considered myself to be an achiever: good student, good athlete—and as a Marine I had accumulated a file of good fitness reports and a combat record in Vietnam that included a Silver Star. I assumed that I would make bird colonel and retire after a full thirty-year career, at least. To get stopped two promotions shy of that goal really knocked the wind out of my sails. I still can't figure out what happened, what I did wrong. Maybe I didn't do *anything* wrong, if you think about it. Of all the majors now in the Corps, only about half are going to make lieutenant colonel, and only half of them are going to make full colonel. So the chances are one in four. The other three majors can't all be failures. A lot of good people have to be passed over.

"I could rationalize all I wanted, but that didn't take away the pain of seeing my contemporaries move on to better jobs and higher pay while a clerk at Headquarters Marine Corps was putting a 'P-1' tag on my service record. I felt branded. There was always a chance of getting picked up by a later selection board, but those odds got extremely long very quickly, and—barring some dramatic development—whatever caused you to fail selection in the first place would still be there in the record to be examined by the next promotion board. After the second pass over the following year (I could visualize that clerk switching the tag to 'P-2') I began to experience something new: People younger than me now were senior to me. I was really hurting, but I couldn't let it show.

"Then before I knew it, that clerk was switching the tag to 'P-3.' Three strikes and out. By law, I had to retire after twenty years' service—ten years ahead of my plan. There was no way to stay on the team I had devoted my entire adult life to."

"George never talked to me about these feelings," Susan said. "He just shut down, almost overnight. It wasn't until our summit meeting that he finally told me he felt like a failure and was sure that I had to think less of him for not getting promoted. But that had never entered my mind. Sure, I was disappointed, too, but think less of George—never! I had been around long enough to understand the system, and we had seen others in the same boat. Of course, we never figured that it would happen to us.

"Another thing we weren't prepared for was the strain that the promotion system put on our long-term friendships, as well as our marriage. Old friends who are still on the way up would feel awkward and embarrassed, and would avoid speaking to us because they didn't quite know what to say. It's easy to say 'Congratulations!' to someone; it's much harder to say 'We know how disappointed you must be, and we're here for you.'

"That new silence really hurt. We weren't looking for fancy speeches—just a few kind words and a little support. Getting passed over can be like a death in the family, for some. You can always use some support while you grieve, until you get your life back together and move on."

"I managed to hide my feelings," said George. "I hid them at work, I hid them from Susan, and I even hid them from myself— even though I was churning inside. Subconsciously, I saw myself as a loser, after being a winner all my life. And I was starting to act like a loser—surly, resentful, short-sighted. A lot of anger was building up in me."

HOUSECLEANING TIME

"And your summit meeting brought all this out?" I asked.

"You bet. Susan really got things started. All our problems didn't melt away overnight, but we had taken the first step in identifying and solving them. And I knew that she was still on my side, despite a couple of miserable years I had given her. On the other hand, I still had some tough stuff to deal with."

"Like what?"

"I had some closets to clean out. The first one was full of my angry and confused feelings. I still hadn't forgiven the Marine Corps for passing me over. It was like holding a grudge against a blood brother, and it was tearing me up. I was sarcastic and critical of nearly everything and everybody—including Susan and the kids, the very people on this earth I care about most.

"The next closet was full of fear. Marines are supposed to be fearless, but I was scared stiff of the world outside. I just couldn't relate to the business world and the people in it—even my friends from college or my home town. Compared with the order and discipline I was used to, the real world was shaky and flaky. I wanted no part of junk bonds, layoffs, Chapter Elevens, or leveraged buyouts. I couldn't see myself selling anything—stocks, insurance, or widgets—and I didn't want to spend the rest of my days strapped to a chair on the twentieth floor of some high-rise office building. I just didn't want to deal with any of the horrors of life after the Marine Corps.

"So I froze at the switch. I kept postponing the decisions and preparations I needed to make. I even found myself praying for a war to start, so I could stay in the Marines longer. The fear I was feeling led naturally to indecision and procrastination. My self-doubt filled a third closet—one I definitely had to clean out.

"In time, it became clear that the first thing I had to do was let go of my anger and stop blaming the Marine Corps for my situation. Then, once I accepted the fact that I would have to start a new life, no matter what, I could get off my duff and do something about those generalized anxieties. I could bring them into focus and beat them down with solid information and common sense, one by one. Once I managed to get myself jump started, I began to feel good about things again. Maybe my old gunnery sergeant, who kept saying 'Do *something*—even if it's wrong!' was on to one of life's basic truths.''

"That was some heavy-duty closet cleaning," I said. "What else did you have to do?"

GETTING READY TO PUNCH OUT

"Well, we took your seminar advice, and each of us made a list of things that had to be done in the seven months or so before I left the Marines, so we could leave with a clean slate. We compared lists, and used them to come up with a set of short-term goals. Nothing happened overnight. We just kept chipping away at the list, a day at a time, while we tried to answer the two big questions.''

''Which were?''

''Where to live . . . and what to do?''

''What brought you to Chicago?''

''We kind of backed into it. Our very highest priority was to find the best school situation for Sally. Her disability is not severe enough to make her permanently dependent. If she receives proper training, she should be able to carve out her own life, working and living in a supervised environment—and within five years or so. We did some checking and soon found that Chicago had both the excellent training programs and the supervised work facilities that we were looking for.

''We also wanted to live close to family, but not right on top of them. Susan's parents live in Milwaukee, some ninety miles away—which is just about right. Chicago was a good fit.''

LOOKING FOR THE CLUES

This was getting exciting. ''How did you find your new careers?'' I asked. ''You couldn't have backed into *them*.''

Susan spoke up. ''We both had careers staring us in the face, but we had to look into every corner of our lives to find the clues. George's first clue should have jumped right out at us, but it took us a while to catch on. You see, George has a green thumb. He always thought of horticulture as a hobby, but when we started checking, we found that it was really an avocation. He majored in biology, concentrating on botany, in college. Everywhere we went, we had the neighborhood's best-looking lawn and garden. He loved to take Scout troops on nature trips. On recruiting duty in Iowa, he spent his spare time at Lou Jolly's farm, driving a tractor to unwind and shooting the breeze with the farmers about crops the way others would talk about cars or sports.

"Testing gave us another set of clues. The tests George took during your seminar showed his high interest in nature and agriculture, as well as science and math—and his low interest in the business world. The tests also gave him high marks in the 'social' field, which pointed toward a teaching career.

"The teaching possibility really moved front and center when we looked at some of George's favorite and less-favorite duty tours as a Marine. One of the favorites was his tour as an instructor at the Landing Force Training Command, near Norfolk."

"I loved that tour," George broke in. "I really looked forward to going to work each day. I found that I could take serial assignment tables and other dry-as-dust amphibious planning documents and make them come to life for the students.

"So we did some more homework. After contacting some placement offices, I found that the demand for horticulture graduates generally exceeded the supply. They were yelling for green thumbs in the private sector—seed, fertilizer, plant, and landscape companies—and in government: municipalities, state, and federal. The field I loved—but never thought about—was wide open."

Susan again—"Now we knew two things: We wanted to move to Chicago, and George wanted to do something connected with horticulture. He was initially leaning toward teaching, but still wanted to check out the other options.

GOING TO THE SCENE

"The next logical step was a week-long visit to the Chicago area. We did as much advance work as possible with letters and phone calls. We tried a relocation firm, which proved to be a smart idea. They narrowed down our housing needs, located some good schools for Sally, and even gave us some good employment contacts. George was able to interview with two companies in his field, and visit four public-school systems and one private school, which proved to be a mixed blessing.

"How come?" I asked.

George answered. "My military background was generally a plus for teaching. They liked structure, discipline, and organizational ability. But they also wanted educational certificates and advanced degrees, which I could have lined up if I hadn't wasted so much time grieving about being passed over.

"I wound up working for a landscape architectural firm, on a part-time basis. We did some interesting stuff—a theme park and golf course, as well as several office complexes and housing developments. I also did substitute teaching, in three different school systems."

"*Two* part-time careers?"

"Three, actually. I was going to school at night to get my masters and my teaching credentials."

"How long did you keep that up?"

"A good year and a half—until I got the job I wanted. Of those three schools where I subbed, I had one clear favorite, and always made myself available when they called. Besides teaching, I helped out with the school's track and cross-country teams, volunteered to lead two field trips, and made a formal course-improvement proposal to the principal. For a substitute teacher, I had pretty high visibility at that school. When the regular biology teacher left one spring because of her husband's business transfer, I was able to finish out the school year—and accept a full-time position for the fall term."

"What did you do about your other business—the landscape architecture work?"

"I'm working both jobs. They complement each other, and keep me from getting into a rut. Last summer, I had a special landscaping project in Wisconsin. The whole family went and we turned it into a long vacation."

We laughed our way through dinner, reminiscing about Camp

Lejeune, but I still hadn't heard Susan's story, and I really wanted to know how she had come through all of this.

"Susan, you've been glowing all evening. What's been going on with you?"

"Well, the things I'm doing right now seem right for me, and it all has something to do with learning to set goals, both short-term and long-term ones. Somebody once said that if you don't know where you are going, any road will take you there. I was getting tired of living like that. So I set some goals.

"My first goal was to put together a decent résumé. As a Marine Corps wife, I had done a lot of unpaid volunteer work for Navy Relief, Red Cross, and other civic projects. When we lived in civilian communities, either adjacent to military bases or on independent duty far removed from them, the long-term residents could see us coming. They knew that we were a reasonably efficient, high-energy source of talent—eager to please during a typical three-year stay in the community and available to work with their civic associations, Scout troops, or whatever. So we were usually invited early on to be committee chairmen while the pillars of the community served on the boards of directors and voted up or down on what we were doing. No big thing—that's just the way things work. But the result, in terms of my own experience, was a string of solid accomplishments: organizing fund drives, managing budgets, directing projects, supervising, troubleshooting—in general, attending to a great many details and solving a variety of problems.

"At the library, I found a book that had sample résumés of heavy hitters—both men and women—in the business world. They were getting paid megabucks for doing the same things I did: organizing, managing, recruiting, promoting. The only difference was that they did those things for generous salaries and benefits. Once I recognized this sameness of experience, I began to grow more and more confident that I could compete in the workplace—in a fast-moving office, to be more specific.

"After our exploratory trip to Chicago, with three-and-a-half months left to go before George's retirement, I began to zero in on that area. We subscribed to a Chicago newspaper, to track the local job market through the classified and business sections. Things were getting interesting.

"Meanwhile, a friend arranged for me to spend a day with the administrative staff of a large medical clinic in North Carolina's Raleigh-Durham area. It was hectic, but I loved it! The chief administrator was generous with her time, and spelled out the skills I would need to break in—the most critical being computer skills.

"My heart sank. I had never worked with computers. Like George, I started to kick myself for losing years of time that could have been used in getting smart. The clinic administrator recommended a computer course that would give me the basics. I took it and plugged away. As my skills increased, so did my confidence. I finally worked up enough nerve to send out about twenty résumés to Chicago-area firms, just to test the water.

"The positive response floored me. Somebody really wanted me! I turned into a real networker, in touch with every friend I ever had in the Chicago area, to figure out what to do. I signed on with a large and growing physicians' practice—four doctors and a staff of seven. At first, I processed claims and did other go-fer jobs. But I became the assistant administrator within two years, and have since been offered (and taken) the chief administrator's job. We now have two offices, seven doctors, and a staff of eleven. The health-care field is booming.

"The real beauty is," Susan continued, "this field is wide open to men and women of all ranks who are coming out of military service. Health-care facilities exist everywhere. I started at the bottom, with no college degree, no experience, and a minimal starting salary. Now I'm a manager, with a decent salary and additional earnings based on an incentive plan that keys on the profitability of the office. That's not too shabby. No wonder I feel good about things."

PAYING THE FREIGHT

I generally steer clear of financial questions during my seminars, unless asked directly. But I really wanted to know how George and Susan managed to swing their deal. So I went ahead and asked.

George jumped in. "We made some money by selling our house in North Carolina, and also had to dip into our very modest savings to get the down payment for this house. We figured that my retirement pay would cover mortgage and taxes on this place, and that we could supplement my early civilian-job salary with up to a thousand dollars a month from savings, if that became necessary. I'll be frank—we had to live very close to the wire for a year and a half. A family night out meant a trip to a fast-food place.

"In terms of the house, we bought a basic place in a central location—and when we had the money, we expanded. The family room we just enjoyed is an annex to the basic house. Now that we have established ourselves here, I expect that we will continue to grow, as we see fit."

GETTING IT TOGETHER

George had become quiet and reflective. "I wouldn't trade my years in the active-duty Marine Corps for anything else in the world. They were terrific years, and they gave me experience and a quiet self-confidence that have really helped me in the civilian world. Sure, I had my slump and a period of self-doubt, but thanks to Susan, and you, and a great many others, I managed to snap out of it before I left active service.

"One of the things that helped was overhearing a first sergeant counsel one of his young Marines:

You have been telling me all the things that are wrong in your life. Now, start telling me what you are doing to correct them.

"Once I caught on to that, I was ready to go full steam up to the finish line, ready for the excitement of the days ahead. I was ready to start Phase II of my life.

"But listen—we've talked your ear off, and we have plenty of time. The way it's snowing, you won't be going anywhere anytime soon. So why don't I just switch on the tube? The Bulls are playing the Detroit Pistons tonight. The start was delayed some by the snowstorm, but they ought to be going at it pretty hard by now."

2

....

TAKING STOCK

Couples like George and Susan are serving today at posts and stations all over the world. The one thing they have in common is that—sooner or later—all of them will have to cross the bridge into retirement. And for most, "retirement" actually means a second career—or a series of jobs that may or may not add up to a real career.

For more than a decade, I have seen many in the profession of arms—from corporals to admirals—arrive at that bridge. Some get there with their personal affairs in order, with well-thought-out career plans, and even with good jobs awaiting them on the other side. Others arrive with their lives and health in pieces, no plans for the future, and no opportunities on the horizon.

If you are breezing along in the fast lane at the moment, with, say, a guarantee of a good job in CivLand,* stick around anyway. In the following chapters, you might pick up a few pointers about developing staying power—something that can be very much under your control.

If, on the other hand, you are sputtering along on two cylinders through a low-hanging fog, don't panic. Stay with me. No matter

---

*The Great Outside, where people march out of step, wear funny clothes, and need haircuts.

how impossible things may seem at the moment, you can turn them around. In my business experience, I have interviewed and screened thousands of job seekers. I have been party to the final hiring decisions for hundreds of those. I can tell you two things:

❯ *Employers often zero in on personal qualities that are not easily displayed on résumés or in interviews.* Once, as national sales manager for a *Fortune*-500 company, I narrowed an executive search—for a key management position in the Northwest—down to two candidates. One was clearly superior in terms of work and educational background. He had five more years' experience in sales, for openers. Nevertheless, after extensive probing, I chose the less-experienced candidate. At age eighteen, he had become a head of household, owing to the sudden death of his parents. While caring for his sister and his ailing grandparents, he managed to join the Naval Reserve and attend college at the same time. This showed me a strong sense of responsibility, maturity, good judgment, and depth of character. To me, his leadership potential acquired through his Navy service more than made up for his lack of sales experience. I was not looking for a supersalesman; I was looking for a leader of salesmen. Fortunately, the service-connected leadership skills were revealed during the job search. Far too often, such qualities are not brought forth at the right time, and everybody loses. This book will keep that from happening to you.

❯ *Your attitude is all important.* You might not be happy about your present situation, especially if circumstances are forcing you to leave military service. You might be bitter, resentful, or cynical about what life has dealt you. Whoa! Just remember that while nobody experiences life as a series of tailor-made situations, everyone can tailor his or her attitude. Sooner or later a negative attitude will kill you in your search for that second career. When interviewing job candidates, I always probe to find out how they have dealt with setbacks, disappointments, and even failures in their lives. Failures are important! No prospective employer expects a straight-A record, but nearly all of them want to know if you can handle a crisis—or even take a licking—bounce back, and move resolutely forward. The ability to deal with adversity is a measure of maturity.

ESTABLISHING YOUR MINDSET

After twenty or more years of hard soldiering, it may be natural to think of retirement from military service as the end of a personal era, maybe even the end of one's primary life work. The reality is that "retirement" can actually mean entering a new phase of life's work, perhaps one that could last even longer than Phase I. An Army sergeant major from Fort Bragg put his own twist on the transition by comparing it to a halftime break in the locker room— time to regroup, to evaluate his own play during the first half, update his game plan, and come out like a hard charger for the second half.

The regrouping process is *essential*. Before you can begin a meaningful self-inventory or take any other of the sequential steps into a Phase II career, you need to identify any excess emotional baggage you may be carrying—and deal with it. In most cases, this is easier said than done, because it means altering habits and relationships that may have existed for years. It may involve professional help, anywhere from counseling to therapy. And it may take a long time, with at best a partial rate of success—life is never tidy. But the effort absolutely must be made, because the job applicant with a sour or cynical attitude will reveal it sooner or later, and will not survive the job-interview process. Who wants to hire anyone with a chip on his shoulder?

Regrouping generally involves six key areas of life:

❯*Family.* This was the starting point, at Susan's initiative, for the new life that George and Susan eventually found. Other aspects of life—friends, acquaintances, power, influence—will ebb and flow, but family is supposed to be the place where the door is always open, whether to share your triumphs or to help you lick your wounds. The logical starting place to mend your relationships is under the roof you share with your immediate family. Then go to work on the extended family. Examine each relationship. Does anything need fixing? Then fix it. Such tough work will make everyone feel better.

Why am I spending all this time telling you that charity begins at home, when your main concern at this point is putting food on the table for that same home? As one corporate vice-president once told me, firms with a close-teamwork approach tend to examine family relationships in their evaluation of applicants, as a predictor of team-building skills. If they are going to look, so should you.

❯*Friends.* If you are leaving the service under less-than-hoped-for conditions, you may have some former friends out there who need forgiving—for your sake, not theirs. They could range from the associate who once dropped a dime on you to the former CO who killed you with faint praise on a crucial report of fitness or efficiency. Your hurt may go all the way to the bone. But the best way to free yourself is to truly forgive those people and tell them so directly. Take them to lunch, as I did to straighten things out with George. It may be the hardest thing you've ever done. But it may be one of the best things you've ever done.

❯*Health.* The armed services demand top physical conditioning, and back up their demand with comprehensive medical care—for those on active duty. Once retired, however, you no longer get to step to the head of the line. In fact, you may be asked—politely, of course—to step to the rear or even out of the line. So if you know of a health problem that needs fixing, get it treated while you are still on active duty. It's time to drop the cops-and-robbers game with the medics, who have always had the power to deny you choice assignments with a ''medically disqualified'' stamp in your service record. They can't block your retirement for medical reasons, except to delay your separation date long enough to send you out with a clean bill of health. So fix whatever is wrong—from a blown-out knee to substance dependence to mental or emotional problems—service related or not, while you can still step to the head of the line as an active-duty patient. Now is not the time to cling to the personal zero-defects syndrome. Don't be too proud to ask for help, when it's needed.

❯*Finances.* As your research deepens into careers that are truly driven by your interests—and not primarily by the prospect of financial reward, although security is always a consideration—some bean counting is in order. After adding up the figures, you may find that you will not have immediate access to the career of your choice. Expensive schooling or training may be required. Starting salaries may be too low, in light of your other financial commitments. Or, if you are thinking of being your own boss, the initial capital investment requirement may be too high. If such is the case, don't despair. Roughly 60 percent of those leaving military service encounter financial barriers at the outset. Those who start earlier in planning their careers sometimes can accumulate savings or line up loans to start up their own businesses or franchises as soon as they step outside the gate; others have to bide their time and create their own opportunities farther down the line, with patience, careful planning, and even an occasional flash of creativity. At critical moments, the advice of an expert financial counselor might be enough to put them over the top.

For example, take the case of Elliott, who had left the Air Force after eight years' service and entered the business world in Phoenix. After four years as a trainee and junior executive, he began to yearn for independence. He saw a future in fast-food franchising, and began to plan ways to come up with the large initial investment required. Nothing seemed to work; he kept coming up short. Finally, he was able to bring together a key representative from the franchise parent company, a banker, and a trusted financial consultant. Together, they worked something out. Elliott currently owns two locations, and is working toward ownership of a third.

❯*Spirituality.* "There are no atheists in foxholes," the saying goes, and certainly we are dealing with severe stress and uncertainty at transition time that may approach some of the strains of combat. But a foxhole mentality is not what we're after. In fact, I much prefer to believe in something a Navy chaplain said in Vietnam: ''There are plenty of atheists in foxholes, but there aren't many atheists back at Charlie Med,'' where the medical battalion's surgeons worked tirelessly to save the severely wounded. There, a spiritual experience—in which a calmness of faith replaces the free-floating anxiety that prolonged exposure to danger and death brings—was more likely to occur, for more people, than on the battlefield itself.

Husbands and wives who have found such moments of serenity together are better equipped to weather the storms of career transition than those who have not—because they know that fear, doubt, and uncertainty, while inescapable at times, are not their lifetime sentence. At the outset of the transition period, if time permits, nearly every couple can benefit from a getaway weekend, where they can find the quiet and freedom from distraction they need to discuss and anticipate their new life together. This can take place at their own favorite vacation spot or perhaps at a spiritual retreat center, in a visit arranged through their church or synagogue. The change in outlook this time-out period can inspire is often quite dramatic.

> *Career.* Your immediate need may be to find a high-paying job, but your long-term focus should be on a career—something new and quite different from your past military experience. In even the most freewheeling military careers, the choices are relatively limited. Oh, there may be some dickering with personnel assignment officers about which new assignments are more career enhancing, and some adjustments in timing to let junior finish the ninth grade in his old school, but there is no question that the System dictates career patterns and generally calls the shots.

By contrast, this ''second'' career is filled with real choices— beginning with where you want to live and what you really want to do, and progressing through the goals and dreams you want to fulfill. As many as 65 to 70 percent of your future waking hours will be spent in your new career—on the job, going to and from, and just thinking about it. That's too much of your valuable time to waste doing something you can't stand. You need to look ahead, at a number of career fields, before settling on the one you will pursue.

But first, you need to take a long look into the past.

THE INVENTORY

The best way to get where you're going is to truly understand where you've been. You need to lay a foundation of self-aware-ness that encompasses your experiences, your accomplishments (and lack thereof), your abilities, and your skills. Next, you must factor in your interests, needs, and dreams. If you do this honestly (which may involve some pain, at times), and patiently, and meth-odically:

> You will know more about yourself than ever before;
> You will have assembled the ingredients of a very strong résumé;
> You will have what it takes to do well in any job interview—poise, self-confidence, and a clear sense of direction;
> And you will be capable of making the right calls, picking the job and career situations that will be right for you.

Let me say it up front: *There are no shortcuts in this process.* You will only be shortchanging yourself. The maxim, "No pain, no gain," definitely applies here. Consider the process I am about to take you through as something like a long-distance run—a jaunt through your life. The need to warm up makes the first mile or two the toughest part of this self-inventory. But once you have organ-ized your documents and warmed to the task, you can settle in for a long run at a comfortable pace, collecting new insights about yourself along the way.

Just as running with a partner makes a workout easier, the in-ventory process works best when you *pick someone to be account-able to*—a spouse, family member, or friend who knows you well and who will help you through those times when you find it difficult to be completely objective about yourself. Husband-and-wife teams are ideal for this, because they both need help in working through the inventory process, and because both have a stake in attaining a realistic, honest outcome.

To get started, you need only a pair of manila file folders, to hold a variety of notes and work sheets. The first folder can be marked ''Wheel.'' Consider the six major elements of life described earlier in this chapter as spokes of a wheel that need to be checked and tightened throughout the process, to ensure the smoothest possible journey across the bridge. Some spokes (e.g., family, friends, health) can be worked on without delay; others (e.g., financial, career) cannot be started until later. But all are in need of continuous attention and tightening throughout the process—and the ''Wheel'' file is your best way of keeping tabs on informal and formal conferences and appointments, and scheduling emotional maintenance, whenever it is needed.

The mainstay of the second file—''Inventory''—is a work sheet that covers your experience, accomplishments, and skills (see facing page for a useful format). For best results, you need to focus on each military assignment or position held, beginning with the most recent, and working—using a page or more for each assignment—all the way back to day one. If you have maintained a file of fitness reports, efficiency reports, or other performance evaluations—or if you can still obtain a set of these reports or a computer printout of your career markings from your parent service headquarters—so much the better. Look for *trends* in these reports— numerical markings in certain categories that are consistently high or low, and written comments by different reporting seniors that tend to stress the same points about your performance—as well as the dates and places of specific duties you have performed. These will lessen your reliance on your own memory and give you a better picture of your performance as others saw it. If such files are not available, you will have to probe, and dig, and soul search all the harder for decent results. Whatever you do, don't rush through this part. You are looking for your strengths, perhaps some that have been hidden over the years. But take a good look at the chaff and weeds that sometime come up with the wheat, because the ability to recognize and understand our weaknesses is a source of strength in itself. If you have had a problem staying organized or staying focused on long-term goals, you can learn about methods and systems designed to help you keep your act together with more skill. If you have stumbled because of low aptitude in certain areas, you should be clearly aware of such pitfalls so you can steer clear of them in the future. It's no weakness to acknowledge areas where you don't "have it." That's just being smart.

In more than twenty years of corporate life, executive recruiting, and career transition work, I have reviewed thousands of résumés and interviewed hundreds of people. The true standouts that I remember best came across not as perfect candidates but as people *who knew who they were*—warts and all. In writing and in person, they were sharp and well focused, and this seemed to give them confidence in themselves. But this self-awareness did not come naturally. Almost every one of them had worked to attain it, to get a firm grip on what they had to offer any prospective employer. They didn't lose opportunities because their experience, accomplishments, and skills somehow failed to come across.

So let's start the inventory process, with our work sheet (Figure 1).

Experience.

Begin with the most recent military assignment and work backward, all the way back to day one. Use a separate sheet (more, if needed) for each billet, task, or experience—even a one-week school might have particular significance. The most recent assignments will probably have the most food for thought and will be the easiest to recall, but don't shortchange the ones further back. Push your memory harder. There might be some real gems of insight buried in that great tour you had as a motor-transport instructor many years ago, or in the recruiting tour in Iowa that turned out to be such a disaster

Figure 1.

EAS WORK-SHEET
(Experience, Accomplishments, Skills)

Position/Title:

Location/Unit:

Inclusive dates:

Supervisory? How many?:

Experience—What did I actually do?:

Accomplishments—What did I actually achieve?:

Skills—What abilities did I actually use or acquire?:

What did I like about the assignment? What did I dislike?:

How well did I do? Any special recognition?

Other Comments:

because you were slow in getting your territory organized. You need all the pieces to put the puzzle together.

Accomplishments.

As you fill out this section, imagine that you are writing a fitness report on yourself, and your next promotion depends on it (actually, the rest of your life may depend upon the outcome of this entire process). Don't exaggerate—this is an exercise in self-knowledge, not self-deception—but avoid undue modesty, which also is a way of fooling yourself. You may have been too busy at the time to reflect on what you actually were accomplishing. (As the old Pentagon adage says: "When you're up to your eyebrows in alligators, you sometimes tend to forget that your original purpose was to drain the swamp.") Upon reflection, you may find that you did more than you realized at the time.

The best way to list and analyze your accomplishments is to write a separate statement for each one. Each statement should have an action verb and should cite a benefit or contribution to the organization. Wherever possible, *quantify* the benefit, because most civilian firms are interested in people who can put bigger and bigger numbers on the bottom line.

Here are some sample accomplishment statements:

> Reorganized base recreational activities, resulting in more efficient use of staff, increased availability of athletic equipment, and a cost savings of 22 percent.
> Exceeded recruiting quotas by 16 percent over a two-year period in a two-state Midwestern region.
> Revised maintenance procedures for heavy trucks, resulting in a 29 percent drop in the vehicle deadline rate.
> Conducted studies of time-sharing terminals and telephone systems that led to savings of 58 percent per year.

You may find yourself rewriting your accomplishment statements several times, to get them just right. The extra effort will be well spent. I cannot overstress the importance of clear, crisp statements, for some of them will find their way into your résumé and, in time, may become focal points of your interviews.

See Figure 2 for some additional sample action verbs.

Figure 2.

SAMPLE ACTION VERBS

Achieved	Eliminated	Researched
Administered	Expanded	Sparked
Analyzed	Installed	Streamlined
Built	Improvised	Trained
Conceived	Motivated	Transferred
Consolidated	Negotiated	Translated
Coordinated	Planned	Trimmed
Cut	Processed	Traced
Delegated	Proposed	Unified
Designed	Purchased	Verified
Directed	Recruited	Won
Doubled	Reduced	Wrote

Skills.

Your accomplishments are in large measure a reflection of your skills, some of which you brought with you into military service and some of which you acquired along the way. You may be putting some of these skills (e.g., administrative or managerial) into daily use, while others (e.g., computer programming) may be sitting on the shelf, waiting to reemerge another day. As you tackle this part of your EAS work sheet, you will be clearing out your warehouse of talents and putting them on display. You probably will be pleasantly surprised at the size of your collection.

Your skills fall into three basic categories:

❯ *Functional skills* are related to or acquired within a variety of organizational functions—e.g., personnel, electronic data processing, warehousing, finance, cooking, marketing.

> *Technical skills* are acquired through specialized education or work experience—e.g., clerical, mathematical, machinery, manual, computer, writing.
> *Administrative and managerial skills* are essential to organizational health—e.g., directing, innovating, creating, organizing, analyzing, delegating, problem solving, planning.

Over the course of a military career, you have received exceptional training and education in both tangible and intangible skills—everything from office management to systems analysis. In addition, you have undoubtedly acquired and reinforced some exceptional personal traits (for example, responsibility and attention to detail), to an extent not normally found in the general population. In combination, these skills and traits can add spark to any organization. Employers love them, and get very interested when they emerge during interviews.

As you walk back through your military career, assignment by assignment, recall which of these traits came through strongest or had a particular bearing on your accomplishments:

> A high level of self-discipline. There must have been times when this made a difference. You'd better believe that employers look for this quality.
> A strong work ethic. This is tied closely to discipline. You will see a task through to its conclusion.
> Willingness to accept responsibility and accountability. From day one, you were given more responsibility (and accountability) than most of your civilian counterparts.
> Honesty and integrity, demonstrated in ethical conduct. From the savings-and-loan industry to Wall Street—is it any wonder that ethics consulting is now a thriving business? Despite an occasional procurement-scandal headline, the armed services are generally respected as being clean—a plus for military employment seekers.
> Physical fitness and appearance. Almost a given, for anyone used to standing and conducting inspections.
> Forehandedness. The habit of planning and thinking ahead to min-

imize problems is almost second nature to military professionals, and is a much-in-demand trait in business and industry, where avoidable screwups can take big dollars away from the bottom line.

> Practicality and attention to detail. These go with forehandedness. Sloppy planning can cost lives in the military; it costs careers and fortunes in business.

> Innovation and creativity. Another strong suit for those who are able to overcome adversity with a "field expedient" when one is needed.

> Extensive education and training. In addition to formal schooling, you probably have a wide variety of on-the-job experience in your knapsack. Such training opportunities also should have helped you develop exceptional oral and written communications skills, which also translate into dollars for the businessman.

> Ability to make courageous decisions. This includes the moral courage to buck the conventional wisdom and do what's right, as well as the physical courage required on the battlefield.

> Steadiness under pressure; perseverance. This is a hallmark of military service, from the first day of recruit training on. The challenges and the nerve-wracking deadlines of business and industry should not be too much for anyone who has succeeded in a pressure-filled career.

> Dedication and loyalty. Every corporate head and businessman dreams of having such employees.

> Understanding of bureaucracy. If you've ever had a tour in the Pentagon or on a high-level staff, you have probably helped write the book on bureaucratic chaos. Many potential employers need help in cutting through the maze—and they will pay well for expert assistance.

> High-tech familiarity. Anyone with hands-on experience is marketable.

> Capability for motivational leadership. In addition to formal command experience, the armed forces demand leadership from the small-unit level on up. Henry Ford once said that he would pay more for good leadership than any other quality. By inspiring their

subordinates and taking care of them, experienced leaders strengthen their organizations while providing enthusiasm and vision—all of which shows up on the bottom line. Serving in leadership positions also may have helped you develop exceptional oral and written communications skills, which also translate into bottom-line dollars for the businessman.

The key point behind this inventory taking is the need for you to become articulate in identifying your experience, accomplishments, and skills—and in relating them to an employer's needs. This inspires confidence—in both you and the employer—that you will be able to handle anything that lands on your plate.

In going through your track record, all the way back to your first race, don't be discouraged by the low points you might find. What's important is what you learn from setbacks and failure. Beyond that, leave the past to the historians and focus your attention on the future.

3

MAKING CHOICES AND
SETTING PRIORITIES

Okay—you've worked your way through the hard part, the of-ten-painful soul-searching. Now it's time to have some fun, and set about choosing what you want to do for the rest of your working days.

Throughout your military service, you have been called upon to make sound and timely decisions. Yet most of your career-management choices have been made for you. By and large, you have been told where and when to report for duty. Those folks in personnel may have tried to take care of your needs and interests, but everyone knows that in a crunch the needs of the service come first.

Now it's your turn. For most, the number of career choices available after military service is dizzying. In selecting among the possibilities, you should take into account your interests, needs, and dreams.

INTERESTS

Let's go back to your work sheets, with their detailed breakout of your experience and skills. If you are like most others, your military service has given you a wide range of skills in a variety of assignments. Which did you enjoy most? Do you like the things you are doing today better than those you were doing three years ago? How about ten years ago? Have the things you enjoy most been connected more closely to your primary duties, or to secondary or additional duties? The type of satisfaction (and the *amount* of satisfaction) you derived from your more significant duties may have differed noticeably from the pleasure you found in lesser ones. If so, this should tell you something about inner needs—as well as interests—that need to be fulfilled in your Phase II existence.

Some of your skills and interests may have been developed outside of any formal workplace situation. Consider skill in teaching, for example. Most military professionals spend up to one third of their time in schools of one sort or another, either as students or teachers. In addition, those in leadership positions automatically assume the roles of teacher, counselor, and coach of their subordinates. Teaching is such a natural follow-on profession for so many leaving military service—and the need for their experience, skill, and talent in the field is so great today—that I often find myself cheerleading for that Phase II option. Sometimes teaching can be combined with another skill, as in the case of the Air Force avionics specialist who now teaches at a technical college and has a part-time business as an avionics consultant—enjoying the best of both worlds.

While looking back over your lifetime of skills, talents, and interests, don't forget the recreational ones: photography, music, boating, gardening, automobiles, or care of animals, for example. There may also be avocational interests, such as working in political campaigns or serving in community-based organizations. It's exciting to imagine—and I want you to imagine—ways to draw pay for continuing with the things that you enjoy doing in your spare time.

If possible, review these with someone who has been doing them with you—your spouse, your best friend, your rod-and-gun buddies, as the case may be. They may be able to help you nail down the most enjoyable aspects of the pastimes you share. For example, if your primary goal with your fully automatic thirty-five millimeter camera is getting a decent set of prints to pass around after vacation trips and family reunions, then photography may not be a potential career field for you. On the other hand, if you have set up your own darkroom and have a working knowledge of composition and lighting, you might find great enjoyment in moving into photography on a full-time basis, whether in a store or a studio.

To augment this initial casting about for postretirement areas of interest, think about trying preference testing. Military bases that offer outplacement services through their family counseling centers should be able to provide you with the Strong-Campbell Interest Inventory (SCII), a forty-minute test that is an excellent tool for helping you zero in on your second career, possibly revealing areas of interest beyond your present conscious awareness.

The SCII measures six occupational themes:

› *Realistic.* These folks prefer work with tools, out of doors whenever possible; they would rather deal with things than people. They also tend to be conformists, who are practical, stable, thrifty, and frank in delivering their opinions. Frequently found among farmers, surveyors, carpenters, and electricians.

› *Investigative.* Task oriented, and usually preferring to work alone, these people enjoy solving abstract problems. Variously classified as analytical, methodical, rational, or simply curious, these comparatively reserved individuals often seek advanced positions in such fields as biology, chemistry, medical technology, and anthropology.

› *Artistic.* Preferring to work in settings that permit the highest opportunity for self-expression, these creative people tend to be idealistic, impulsive, intuitive, and often nonconformist. They are happiest working as writers, composers, actors, directors, artists, and set designers, among other things.

› *Social.* People-oriented men and women with a high social component tend to be persuasive, insightful, generous, responsible, and understanding. They gravitate toward careers in teaching, counseling, personnel management, and the clergy.

› *Enterprising.* Quickly growing impatient when subjected to close-detail work for any length of time, these adventurous souls turn their considerable energies and self-confidence toward careers in sales, promotions, and business management, where they can speak out, sell, and lead.

> *Conventional.* These conscientious, conservative, practical, persistent people prefer the highly ordered activities usually associated with office work. They excel as bookkeepers, bankers, and experts in taxes and legal matters, among other things.

In addition to measuring your compatibility with these occupational areas, the Strong-Campbell Interest Inventory will tell you about the strength of your interest in such specific areas as sales, writing, or mechanical work. It also will show how similar (or dissimilar) your interests are to those of people successfully employed in these fields.

After you have narrowed your focus to a relatively few areas of second-career interest, do some follow-up research. In nearly every field, there are bound to be local people on hand who can answer your questions and give you insights into their businesses or professions. A walk through the yellow pages or a city directory or a trip to the chamber of commerce can produce a starter set of names for the beginnings of a network of contacts in your chosen fields. You will generally find that most business and professional people will be flattered by your interest, and—within reason—will give you some of their time. Just be considerate. The middle of tax-preparation season is a poor time to ask for a session with a certified public accountant, for example.

You can begin this type of career research from afar, if any kind of mail service exists. In fact, the impact of an inquiry from a remote spot can be quite powerful. During the Persian Gulf War, a young Marine named Ted wrote personal letters to the heads of a dozen accounting firms in the Houston area. Ted's brother had obtained a list from the yellow pages, then called each firm for the name (double-checking the spelling) of the senior partner. In each letter, Ted said that he hoped to return from Operation Desert Storm and finish his Marine Corps service within a year or so, and he hoped to begin a career in accounting, possibly with that firm. All but one of the partners responded. They loved his resourcefulness and use of humor in describing his situation (he even included a flattened Saudi Arabian sand flea in one letter). The upshot: Ted now works for one of the top accounting firms in Houston.

The lesson here is to make a difficult situation work *for* you, and don't be hesitant to show a sense of humor as you do. Employers will usually pay extra attention to those who demonstrate unusual initiative in contacting them.

In less-remote duty assignments, you can gain practical experience in your field of interest while still serving on active duty. For example, a Navy recruiter on his twilight tour in Florida found time to enroll in photography classes at the local community college, and even to work part-time in a studio. Upon leaving the service, he went to work with a major studio in the Southeast. After three years, he was ready to go into partnership with the owner.

If the demands of your active-duty assignment preclude moonlighting for second-career experience, learn what you can through your own study, either formal or self-administered. Your initial points of contact in the field, or the local librarian, can provide reference material.

As you sample various selections from this smorgasbord of life's choices, keep in mind the fact that 60 to 70 percent of your waking hours will be spent in your new workplace—either on the job, traveling to and from it, or thinking about it. You may not land the perfect job on the first try, but if you do your homework, you will have some desirable alternatives waiting.

NEEDS

Each of us has certain inner needs that must be satisfied in any search for a second career. That is why an officer stationed at Marine Corps Base, Twentynine Palms, California, for example, might derive great *enjoyment* from collateral duties of coaching an intra-

mural basketball team and contributing articles to the base newspaper—but might take even *deeper satisfaction* in his primary
duties, which might involve the testing and evaluation of Marine
infantry battalions in live-fire exercises, and subsequent refinement
of Marine Corps battle doctrine. Even though the work of analyzing
postexercise reports and correlating mounds of statistics often is
tedious, the significance of the work is clear to him, because it
could save the lives of many Marines in battles yet to be fought.
It is the desire to devote oneself to something that truly makes a
difference that has been a major motivating factor for many, if not
most, who have made careers in the armed services.

By retirement time, this drive to play a vital role in national
security may have begun to burn itself out, or at least to transform
itself into an acceptance of other ways of making a difference—
helping others through the teaching or nurturing professions, for
example. But whatever form this internal need takes for you, it must
be accommodated if you are to truly enjoy Phase II. Some companies have done particularly well at meeting such internal needs
of their employees—Apple Computer, for example, whose workers
take great pride in their firm's pioneering high-tech work.

Here are other examples of these deeply felt needs:

❯*Esprit de corps.* The close bonding brought about by dangers
shared and victories won is most likely to be missed by military
professionals. But strong team spirit also thrives in CivLand. Hewlett-Packard and the quick-delivery pizza distributor Domino's,
among others, have excelled in blending individual aspirations into
team goals.

❯*Belief in the product.* One former Army officer had earned a
degree in marketing and had served as the promotion manager of
her college yearbook before entering the service. Creative and
sales-oriented, she found that the assignment that gave her the most
pleasure was a tour of recruiting duty late in her seven-year Army
career. Upon leaving the service, she was delighted to be hired by
a prestigious New York marketing and promotion firm. Then she
found out that her first assignment was to the account of a major

beer company, to come up with ads designed to build brand-name loyalty among college students and other young adults. Her own experiences in school and in the Army had led her to a position strongly against promoting alcohol to young people in their formative years. She had to weigh the upward mobility promised by successful work on this beer account against her personal value system. Her value system won. She changed jobs—and despite the short-term opportunity cost, she was happier for making that move. She stayed in the marketing field, working accounts she felt comfortable with, and is now a midlevel manager with a major pharmaceutical company.

❭ *Creativity*. Even the most office-bound accountant or administrator needs a chance to be creative from time to time—and to be recognized, appreciated, and rewarded for it. Creativity goes far beyond writing plays and composing songs; in a firm, it is most likely to appear in the form of innovative problem solving.

❭ *Individuality*. If an individual must dissemble to be accepted within the company culture, the marriage is not made in heaven. One retiring naval officer lived in dread of spending the rest of his working days in a sincere-suit and power-tie world, encased in a skyscraper somewhere. With a few suggestions from me, and a lot of digging and preparation on his part, he was able to acquire a log cabin building franchise in the Northeast, where he flourishes today. Your own passions may not be as strong as that naval officer's, but you do need to find out what they are. Then you are in a position to check out a company's prevailing customs and attitudes before you join—during the interview process, if not sooner.

DREAMS

Just as your military career had an inevitable end, so will Phase II. Where do you want to be and what do you want to be doing when it's all over and you can truly *retire*?

Maybe the ultimate dream is a house in the country (or at the shore, or in the mountains) where you and your spouse will be surrounded by doting grandchildren on appropriate occasions. Perhaps it's two houses—one where it's warm in the winter and another where it's cool in the summer.

On the other hand, your lifetime dream could be focused on a specific achievement—writing a novel or sailing around the world, for instance—something that needs to be accomplished in the shorter term, while you are still young enough. If you can possibly swing a long-enough break between your military service and Phase II to go after a short-term dream, I heartily recommend it. It could be an important part of gearing down from one life and gearing up for the next—and the odds are that you've certainly earned it.

If you can't afford the luxury of a break between careers, you may be able to arrange a sabbatical from your Phase II employment at some point further down the road, to pursue a lifelong dream. This is a tempting, but limited prospect, however. According to Department of Labor statistics, only 13 percent of U.S. corporations offer sabbatical leaves of absence. Colleges and universities are a lot better at this.

Perhaps the ideal solution may be to blend your Phase II career with your dream, taking the steps necessary to wind up running a country inn in New England or a ski lodge in Colorado. It may mean going to law school, where your classmates will be younger than your own children, then starting up a small-town practice. Or it may mean fulfilling a childhood ambition by buying into a minor-league baseball franchise, in one capacity or another.

In this early brainstorming stage, it's okay to let a lot of blue sky into the process, to ensure that you are giving free rein to your imagination. As these dreams come into sharper focus, however, a bit of preliminary research will be in order. Dreams are seldom risk free, especially in financial terms, so you should begin to gather pertinent information, talking to people who have been where you want to go, for openers. Good advice can whet your enthusiasm; inadequate or inaccurate information can either paralyze you with unreasonable fear or propel you into certain disaster.

To maintain your motivation, you must be able to imagine yourself in the situation of your dreams, and *you must be able to return to that compelling image of the future* whenever you begin to waver. You also have to recognize and accept the hard work that stands between you and your dream, and imagine yourself going through that, as well.

Since you are exploring all corners of your life, why not explore your own dreams, as well? Our great nation has been built on them. You need only to look around to see some great success stories. And since you are looking for a Phase II career that is driven by your interests, why not explore the chance that your dreams and your interests will overlap?

Don't ignore your dreams. Check them out.

Then write them down. At this stage of your self-analysis, you should be able to set up a three-column work sheet. In the first column, list the major areas of experience and skill derived from your Chapter Two work sheets. In the second column, record your major fields of interest, as derived from testing or your own research. Finally, make a third column of your favorite dreams that still seem doable after some initial checking. Do you see any matchups? In two of the columns? Across all three? Consider any such correlations as clues to your future. Keep the three-column work sheet handy, adding new information as it emerges.

DECIDING ON YOUR PRIORITIES

If you have dug into the last chapter and have gone through some serious soul-searching, you have accumulated a lot of information about yourself. Depending upon the degree of self-awareness you began with, much of this information may be new to you—or perhaps you have unearthed some old facts and have held them to a new light. Some of what you've found out may be truly exciting, emerging in the form of long-blocked desires, needs, and dreams that now have reappeared, as if by magic, within the realm of the possible.

The trick now is to organize all that information in ways that will enable you to make those sound and timely decisions required both of military leaders and captains of industry. (Even the truly incompetent, such as some of the referees we see in televised athletic contests, can be taught to *act* in a decisive manner. But there's a major difference between that and making consistently sound decisions with regard to complex issues, after taking into account a welter of data and a number of constantly changing variables.) True decision makers are a rare commodity. And rare means valuable.

Look at the example of a Marine major—veteran of two infantry tours in Vietnam, during which he collected the Navy Cross, among other decorations. Seeking a change of pace, he applied for the highly competitive White House Fellows Program and was selected on his second try. After a year in the rarefield atmosphere at the cabinet level in Washington, D.C., he returned to the Corps and took a look at his future. With the normal luck of the draw, he would have to wait the best part of a decade before getting even a *chance* to command an infantry battalion, the next step up the ladder. He decided to punch out. His military record and Fellows' connections enabled him to win a spot in the New York headquarters of one of the country's leading banks, despite a lack of banking or financial-management experience. Before long, he was a vice-president. He kept moving up the ladder, and has been a senior vice-president for quite a while. When asked about his phenomenal success, he said: "It's simple. They were desperate for someone who could make a decision." Just think of it—this major institution, awash in MBAs, was chronically short of qualified decision makers! Are there any other firms like that?

You bet.

Decision-making research has become big business. A Princeton-based firm that has given decision training to more than two million managers over the years has concluded that U.S. companies employ valid decision-making procedures only 12 percent of the time. In Chicago, the Center for Decision Research concluded several years ago that "Most people are woefully muddled information processors who often stumble along ill-chosen shortcuts to reach bad conclusions.''

Why do I put such emphasis on decision making? Because it is central to the setting of short-, mid-, and long-range goals. Without a goal—a destination—you are doomed to wander in the jungle, instead of finding a clear path out of it. Your deepest desires and dreams must be translated into achievable goals, if they are ever to become reality. And in the process of reaching for your goals, you will be stretched—mentally, emotionally, and physically. In other words, you will grow toward those things you want most from life.

I have talked with many who have had difficulty setting goals and have been drifting through the transition process. A retired Navy machinist's mate said it best: he felt like ''frozen machinery'' when it came to goal setting. What was the cause of his inaction, and that of so many others? Basically, it was a deep-rooted fear of *setting the wrong goals.*

Could such a common fear be unreasonable?

Let's look at the case of the retired Air Force officer I counseled, during his fourth year in CivLand. He was working in his third job since retirement, and was just as miserable there as he had been in the other two. We went back to basics, and determined that his initial inventory of his skills had left a great deal to be desired. Because he had held a number of administrative jobs in the Air Force, he assumed that his Phase II future lay in administration. If he had probed deeper into the written evaluations of his active-duty years, he would have realized that he fell far short of perfection as an administrator. He had real trouble organizing his work, meeting deadlines, and guiding others under his supervision—mostly because he couldn't guide himself very well. To make things worse, stubborn pride kept him from seeking additional training to improve his organizational skills.

He took all these inadequacies out of the gate and into CivLand, landing in a series of administrative positions where he failed every time. Furthermore, he hated what he was doing—enough to change jobs almost yearly!

During our career-counseling sessions, we uncovered the administrative hangup. After he took the Strong-Campbell Interest Inventory test and we went through some in-depth probing, we began to see some strong correlation with the "Social" and "Enterprising" occupational themes. The key to his future emerged from an unexpected spot: an additional-duty assignment, late in the Vietnam War, as a casualty-assistance officer. The wrenching task of helping the survivors of those killed or severely wounded in wartime was one of the most difficult anyone could face. Yet he performed that onerous duty with skill and compassion. Despite the emotional toll, he rated the assignment as a net plus, because of the gratification he derived from his ability to render genuine help where it was desperately needed.

Okay—let's end the suspense. Our man is now a funeral director in Pittsburgh. He is active in civic affairs, specializing in problems of the homeless. And yes—he finally went through a workshop that dealt with organizational skills and has cleaned up that part of his act, as well. Now that he has found his niche, his wife and family are happy, too.

The joy of the family at this successful outcome is much too significant to pass by without a second look. No man or woman is an island. I have seen far too many retirees try to go it alone at transition time, under the mistaken assumption that being "self-sufficient" is doing the right thing for the people around them. Everyone—including the children—should be players, from the outset. Excluding family members from decisions that affect their lives profoundly is an invitation to disaster.

Bringing in the family to the already multifaceted process of selecting a second career may seem to complicate the situation beyond all hope. In reality, however, it simplifies reinforcing the need for the decision maker to set priorities.

In establishing your own priorities, you will be considering the competing claims of three key areas:

❯*Calling and Career.* This will be the driving factor for those who, for whatever reasons, want to become CEOs or—better yet—

to own their own businesses, whatever the size. A priority on career-as-a-calling would also apply to the altruistic individuals who elect to forsake big salaries or the comforts of home—either to become a cleric or counselor to run a leper colony in Bombay, or otherwise dedicate themselves to the service of mankind.

❯ *Compensation.* This *has* to be a major consideration for families that are still struggling with out-of-sight college expenses and killer mortgages. It also causes people to seek salary increases in lieu of other benefits, to build the highest possible base for the (second) retirement package.

❯ *Family and Life-style.* After twenty to thirty years of living like nomads, packing up and moving every three years or so, some folks just want to put down roots somewhere. Empty-nest retirees, in particular—whose adult children are out making their own way in the world—may already find themselves in relatively comfortable circumstances, as they await visits by their grandchildren. They need *jobs* less than they need some type of *meaningful work,* preferably avocations they particularly enjoy that will bring in supplemental income for minor luxuries.

The relative priority of each of these three areas will shift during the lifetimes of most individuals and families, to meet changing needs. At times, the shifts will be made deliberately, in anticipation of a substantial payoff further down the line. Take the case of Dean, the Navy commander who had skippered two destroyers before he hit the twenty-year mark, but still decided to try his hand in CivLand instead of remaining in the service. After successful interviews with a major consumer-products firm, he was told by management that he had just the qualities they sought: leadership, communications and organizational skills, and a strong positive image—*but* he had absolutely no knowledge of their business. The company was willing to take a chance with him, if he would take a chance with them. He would have to start at almost a basic-trainee level, then undergo an accelerated training-and-testing program that might require him to move two or three times in a relatively brief period. He would hold go-fer jobs and work on the shipping lines. He would be working for supervisors some fifteen years younger—roughly equivalent to the ensigns and junior-grade lieutenants who had worked for *him* on board ship—and he would be under intense scrutiny all the while. If he went through all the wickets successfully, he had a good shot at becoming the general manager of one of the firm's many plants.

Dean's wife put her leisure-retirement dreams on hold, and once again paid her dues, supporting her husband. Packing up for short-notice moves was something she had learned to do as a Navy wife, and after she and Dean talked it through, she decided that she was willing to take the risk.

It worked. After three-and-a-half years on trial, Dean was named general manager of a plant in Cincinnati—and his wife finally could measure their big new house for custom-made draperies.

Dean's decision (with his wife's concurrence) to place career considerations temporarily ahead of family, life-style, and compensation carried a bigger risk and a higher payoff, but it is no different in substance than a couple's decision to live in reduced circumstances while one (or both) pursues a graduate degree as a prelude to a business or professional career. Most life situations that call for a rearrangement of priorities, however, are not that stark or clear cut. Many more subtle considerations are involved, and you need a way to ensure that you have taken all of them into account.

SETTING PRIORITIES: A DECISION MODEL

I have found the following decision model, developed from a format used at Harvard University, quite helpful in guiding my clients through their own priority-setting processes—making the combinations of small choices that lead eventually to a major choice in life's work.

Let's get into the model, with a discussion of its major components:

The three major areas affecting career choices (Career, Compensation, and Family and Life-style) have been broken down into a number of subfactors, each of which may be rated on a scale of one to one hundred in terms of their relative importance to you. The total score for all thirty-five factors listed (and any you may wish to add), however, must not exceed one hundred. If only four factors (say, size of the firm, starting salary, educational opportunities, and no overtime) have any significance for you, and each is equally important—each would receive a score of twenty-five and all other factors would receive zeros. At the other extreme, if all thirty-five factors have roughly equal importance for you, they would receive threes and fours, again totaling one hundred. Most of us fall somewhere in between, with a number of zeros reflecting our indifference to certain factors, and our passionate intensity toward other factors reflected in eights and tens. On your first run-through, try marking the factors you care about on a scale of one to ten, without too much concern about hitting the mandatory total of one hundred. Then go back and make the choices and set the priorities you need to bring your score down (or up) to one hundred. You may find yourself scoring some factors higher than ten, as the process unfolds.

The only significance of the numbers themselves is to denote relative priorities. Those who put ten beside "long-term salary" may be as intense about that factor as those who score it twenty-five—they're just intense about more additional factors, as well.

Remember that you are scoring the *relative importance to you* of the various considerations—not making the choices themselves. For example, it doesn't matter at this stage whether you prefer a large or a small company. The point is, rather, that if you have a strong preference (for one *or* the other), your score for "company size" should be relatively high; if you couldn't care less about the size of the company, the score should be zero.

The result should give you a clue about the relative importance of the three major areas to you, and get you thinking about which career characteristics are *mandatory* for you, which are *strongly preferred,* and which are merely *preferred.*

This is not a one-time drill. Pull the decision model out and rework it occasionally. You'll be surprised at the way the numbers keep changing. Over a period of ten years, members of my seminars report massaging this model at intervals ranging from three to twelve months. Most came up with changes—some major, some minor.

For example, a sergeant major who was excited about the prospect of making big money on the outside consistently had big numbers in the "Compensation" category. Over a four-month period, however, two "Family and Life-style" factors began to emerge and tilt the scale—his wife's ongoing career in day-care work and his thirteen-year-old daughter's steady development into a top junior tennis player. He and his wife agreed to split the travel time needed to supervise and encourage their daughter during tournaments away from home. This meant that he had to forgo career training in sales that would have kept him on the road three to five days a week. Instead, he opted for a career in real estate sales, where he could regulate his own schedule.

I work with this model myself. Among other things, it helped me decide to start work on this book, at the expense of some other pending projects. It's always good to *talk* issues through, but there is no substitute for committing them to paper.

A final thought: Be sure to save this "priorities" work-sheet and any updates. In addition to helping guide you toward appropriate job opportunities, it will become invaluable at interview time.

Figure 3.

PRIORITY-SETTING MODEL

CAREER FACTORS

Career Development   *Score*
- Function (e.g., personnel, accounting) _____
- Level (e.g., vice-president, director) _____
- Industry (e.g., manufacturing, services) _____
- Strengths emphasized (e.g., "people" skills) _____
- Weaknesses played down (e.g., no math required) _____

Company
- Size _____
- Prestige (reputation outside the firm) _____
- Professionalism (standards within the firm) _____
- Level of technology used _____
- Type of people employed _____
- Leadership style (authoritarian versus democratic) _____
- Track record on layoffs _____

Personal
- Risk of being fired _____
- Advanced degree opportunity _____

                                           Subtotal _____

COMPENSATION FACTORS

Compensation
- Salary: Initial _____
-              Long-term _____
- Bonus (stock?) potential _____
- Perquisites (e.g., company car) _____
- Benefits package _____
- Promotion path _____
- Fast-track potential _____
- Opportunity to buy this company _____
-             —start own spinoff business _____

                                           Subtotal _____

FAMILY AND LIFE-STYLE FACTORS

Geography
- Home ownership
- Proximity to military base benefits
- Likelihood of subsequent relocation
- Family educational opportunities
- Spouse's career opportunities
- Proximity to extended family
- Cultural opportunities

Time Commitment
- No overtime
- No night work
- No weekend work
- No combination of nights and weekends
- Travel requirements

Intangibles
- Pressure on the job
- Job satisfaction

Subtotal _____

Grand Total _____

In addition to your work sheets from Chapter Two, you now have two working documents to help you keep track of changes in an otherwise kaleidoscopic collection of interests, needs, dreams, and career-determining considerations that must always be prioritized. Keep referring to them and updating them, as your career search begins to come into clearer focus.

4

....

WHAT'S REALLY OUT THERE—AND HOW TO FIND IT

═══════════════════════════

"Now I know how Rip Van Winkle felt," said the veteran artilleryman. "I didn't realize that I had been so isolated from the outside world for more than twenty years, but the world I'm going back into is totally different from the one I left to join the Army. Worse yet, it's different from the world I expected to find outside the gates of Fort Sill. I might as well be starting out on another planet."

A veteran retiring from Virginia's Langley Air Force Base had another common reaction: "I have been watching the outside world closely, but now I see that it's been like watching a football game on television—with the sound turned off. I've generally been able to keep up with the score, but I've missed a lot by not hearing the play-by-play chatter."

You may have been doing your best to keep up—even when deployed to remote areas—but even the most diligent effort along this line cannot match the experience of seeing the business world from the inside of a firm. The view is entirely different.

There is no way to take a comprehensive snapshot of the business world. For one thing, the picture is constantly moving, with currents, crosscurrents, and eddies that make the Colorado River's white-water rapids look like a mill pond. Complicating matters further is the difficulty in getting spin-free reporting about economic conditions, under the ever-present shadow of electioneering, no matter what the year. The "ins" are always trying to put the best face on things, no matter how bad; the "outs" work just as hard to paint a picture more dismal than it ever could be. Worse yet, many mass-media outlets aren't very good at sorting through things in an unbiased way—even when they try.

THE TRENDS

Whatever the difficulties in getting a completely accurate picture, certain facts, trends, and conclusions are inescapable. And after taking a look at them, we can begin the transition process by seeing how you might relate to them and even benefit from some of them. Let's start with the most obvious: the country is on its way out of a recession, but the recovery has been slow and spotty. The economic downturn was not as severe as the one we went through ten years ago—and it was only half as deep as concurrent downturns in Europe and Asia—but it was accompanied by other aberrations that have made its effects more widely felt:

> Deregulation that sent major airlines from boom times to bank-ruptcy, and set the stage for disaster in the savings-and-loan indus-try—which in turn has led to shakiness in the banking industry and still more unpleasant ripple effects.
> A myopic tax "reform" package that deepened the recession and wreaked havoc upon the real estate industry, among others.
> The streamlining of major U.S. corporations, in response to more intense competition both at home and abroad. Over the past decade, the *Fortune* 500 companies have chopped more than 3,500,000 em-ployees from their payrolls, and the process continues.
> Well-publicized instances of fraud, waste, and abuse—in both gov-ernment and industry—and a subsequent focus on ethical reform.
> The end of the Cold War and subsequent drawdown on the De-partment of Defense—a planned reduction of more than one million active-duty, reserve, and civilian members by 1995—and closure of more than seven hundred military bases and installations at home

and overseas. Other nonrecipients of this "peace dividend" are Defense-related industries nearly across the board, whose draw downs and closures are creating pockets of unemployment where affluence once reigned. By the mid-1990s, as many as two million Defense-related workers could be seeking new employment, in additional to the federal employees.

If you've been keeping reasonably current, none of this should come as a shock to you. The thing to remember is that the dismal scene I've just outlined can be broken down into a set of challenges—and challenge creates opportunity, which often comes disguised as hard work.

NO MORE GOLD WATCHES

The days of the automatic thirty-year colonels and captains and sergeants major are long over. Even the leaders who have survived a series of tough selection boards—and who have every right to call their careers successful—face the prospect of leaving the service earlier than planned, "selected out" by early-retirement boards. In a more perfect world, no one would have to endure such an indignity at the end of long years of faithful service. But in a changing world driven by hard fiscal realities, such career-end uncertainty will become the norm. Try not to take it personally. When the money is no longer there, good people have to leave.

The armed services and defense industries are not the only ones to undergo such drastic change. In 1991, for example, International Business Machines—the corporate giant that dominated the computer industry for years by producing very large, high-profit-margin mainframes—stopped growing, for the first time since 1946. Seeing the industry's shift toward personal computers, and the concurrent rise in importance of software and services, Chairman John Akers had earlier set about breaking down IBM's Big Blue into thirteen "Baby Blue" autonomous divisions, to reduce costs while stressing services and customer satisfaction. By 1992, the IBM work force was down by 85,000 from its 1986 peak of 407,000, and layoffs were continuing. Managers dropped from 50,000 to 36,000, and Akers himself was replaced in 1993.

What should all this say to us? Essentially, that a security-driven employee, who dreams of spending a full career with a large firm and retiring with a gold watch and a generous pension, is probably out of luck. A more typical employee might now expect to change jobs at least ten times and change careers as many as three or four times during a lifetime's work. As the armed forces continue adjusting to post-Cold War realities, big business is going through a similar process. None of the now-streamlined *Fortune* 500 companies will ever move back to their former bloated structures. Fully 80 percent of job opportunities will be generated by small businesses of fifty to five hundred employees, while the big boys stay on their enforced diets.

Another factor to take into account is the shrinkage and even disappearance of Defense-related employment opportunities that have traditionally served as options for retiring military personnel. Just a few years ago, before deregulation, the airline industry predicted worldwide expansion of such magnitude that the pool of retiring and resigning military pilots would no longer be able to fill the demand. Today, however, leaving the service early to go after big flying bucks on the outside is a shaky proposition. The same situation holds true for aircraft manufacturing companies, shipyards, and even "beltway-bandit" consulting firms, the last refuge of retiring denizens of the Pentagon.

QUALITY AND ETHICS—HERE'S WHERE YOU COME IN

Out of this discouraging picture of reduced opportunity, however, some rays of hope emerge—for those who can catch them. In the highly competitive atmosphere of downsizing and readjustment, new emphasis is being placed on enlightened management and quality control. A recent survey showed that more than 80 percent of consumers regard quality as more important than price. In 1978, only 30 percent said that. More than forty colleges and universities now offer degrees in quality technology, and close to 90 percent of the largest U.S. industrial corporations have expanded their quality-enhancement programs over the past few years.

Some of the more successful Japanese firms owe much to the theories of an American, Dr. W. Edwards Deming, who encouraged them always to keep the customer in mind and work at continually improving their internal processes to ensure harmony and productivity in the workplace. Packaged as "Total Quality Management," Deming's theories are now being adopted by segments of U.S. industry, including some government facilities that form part of the industrial base. Repackaged as "Total Quality Leadership," they are being introduced to the military's operating forces, as well—as part of a comprehensive, top-down effort to equip the armed forces with the means to do more with less over the long term. The chances are good that you will encounter TQL before you retire, if you haven't already. The more you bring to CivLand in terms of practical application of these new management and leadership techniques, the more valuable you will be to a potential employer. If your command or installation is not implementing TQL, or if you have not attended mandatory TQL training, ask to be assigned to a class. You can get the general picture by reading Deming, but training is required to get a real grasp of this complex concept, which far too often is subject to misinterpretation.

As you may have discovered already, cuts in the work force are rarely matched by cuts in the amount of work to be done. Employers, caught in a squeeze between heightened competition and increased overhead costs (for mandatory employee-benefits packages, among other things) will continue to demand more and more from fewer and fewer workers, many of whom have acquired a comfortable nine-to-five mindset over the years. The result is stress, which is well on its way to becoming the most common disease of the 1990s. A 1991 Northwestern National Life study stated that one of every three U.S. employees gave serious thought to quitting work during 1990, because of job-related stress. Roughly the same number expected to burn out on the job within a year or so. This is serious business. Stress sabotages productivity and increases absenteeism, while leading to other health and emotional problems. From the first day of boot camp or officer-candidate school, you have seen your share of high-stress situations and environments and managed to survive. Some of you even thrive when the going gets roughest. Your ability to bring effective stress-management skills to the workplace, along with innovative ways to tackle the more-with-less syndrome will also enhance your value to future employers. On the other hand, if one of your primary goals in a postmilitary career is a stress-free environment, you must factor that—early—into your assessment of any new job opportunity.

For the past decade or so, the question of corporate and personal ethics has been repeatedly illuminated by high-profile investigations, hearings, and trials. It's enough to make anyone leaving the service—where high standards, despite the exceptions that prove the rule, tend to be enforced—wonder about what kind of jungle is out there. As one Navy couple, preparing to retire in Hawaii, said: "The thing that frightens us most is having to deal with all the fraud and corruption out there. Every time you pick up the newspaper, somebody has ripped off somebody else again."

There is probably less here than meets the eye. The frequency and severity of ethical violations is probably not much different from past decades; it's the reporting and prosecution that have burgeoned. The rules have changed, that's all.

Do corporations have ethical codes? Certainly. About 75 percent of them do, according to the Ethics Resource Center in Washington, D.C. It is interesting that half of these codes were written in the mid-to-late 1970s—the post-Watergate era. Most of these codes state that the integrity of the corporation rests upon the integrity of its individual employees, and you will find that most employees in just about every firm are honorable people with solid standards of conduct.

The system breaks down, whenever it does, after competition

gets heated and some companies are forced to deal with business situations where the honorable course to take is not always obvious. Their stated policies are seldom unethical, but their top leadership can sometimes imply that the end justifies the means in reaching a company objective, and an overzealous subordinate can take that as a license to steal. To an action-oriented military officer or non-commissioned officer, accomplishing the mission at all costs is paramount. In the corporate world, however, taking an objective at all costs could prove to be far too costly—for the individual and for the parent corporation.

The general concern over ethics issues works in your favor. The armed services, despite periodic headline-grabbing embarrassments, still enjoy a clean image as one of the most-admired professions. Industry is looking for military hard chargers to come in and play a tough game, but without penalties for unnecessary roughness. Your inner commitment to high ethical standards will soon be recognized, and it will stand you in good stead.

The MBA program at the University of Pennsylvania's Wharton Business School is one of the nation's best in high finance. Possibly as one consequence of recent Wall Street scandals, however, the Wharton School is shifting its emphasis to produce business leaders—not financiers—of the future.

Their new MBA program will:

> Add greater global perspective
> Place new emphasis on ''people'' skills
> Focus on real-world problem solving
> Foster creativity and innovation.

This should provide a clue about the needs of U.S.—and world—industry of the future. They are looking for broad-vision, people-oriented problem solvers who are not afraid of new ideas and who are willing to roll up their sleeves for hands-on involvement in their divisions, departments, or projects. Add a strong sense of ethics and loyalty, and we have a strong MBA package—courtesy of the armed forces. Your on-the-job MBA training matches that of many schools.

I speak from experience. My first position after active-duty military service was as a marketing trainee with a major consumer-products company. It had a thirteen-month training program, and it hired four trainees that year. The other three had MBAs from leading schools. My postgraduate credentials did not go beyond my military background—but, as I learned later, that background got me hired.

I had no special connections (I learned about the position through a job fair). I was an average student, with no special writing skills. But the company perceived that it could build on skills I brought to it from my Marine Corps experience. The firm had hired a former Army man for the same reasons two years earlier, and he had done quite well with the company.

From your own military experience and earlier soul-searching, you should realize by now that there are some things you do better than most other people. The trick is to match those skills and talents with business opportunities, which often come disguised as problems to be solved. You should be asking yourself questions like these:

❭ Can my Total Quality Leadership training and experience help send more dollars to the bottom line of this firm?

❭ Can I bring order out of the administrative chaos I sense in this company?

❭ Can I help resolve the sticky ethical situation this outfit is saddled with?

❭ Can I pull a group together to accomplish this firm's short-term goals?

❭ Can I rally people to the cause, for a long-term effort?

Military leaders often develop a sixth sense, which alerts them whenever something is not right—either with machinery or with people. The experienced machinist's mate who can ''hear'' trouble brewing in his ship's propulsion system long before a breakdown and the crew chief who knows instantly when one of his aircraft's engines starts running rough are almost stereotypical. Equally commonplace are the truly effective unit leaders who know their troops as well as they know their jobs. Through close observation of the appearance and behavior of their subordinates and a clear notion of their goals and objectives, these leaders know when to apply pressure—and when to relax it—to foster a unit's healthy pride in its ability to accomplish its missions. Such insight cannot be taught in school, but it is valuable in the corporate world, if applied with conviction and decisiveness to solve a company's problems before they get out of hand. If you have that sixth sense—which may be no more than highly developed powers of close observation and common sense, the product of long experience in making things work—let it be known to your prospective employers. Someone who can keep a sensitive finger on a company's pulse always will be in demand.

FINDING THE RIGHT CAREER: THE FIRST STEPS

Despite all the cutbacks and layoffs in government and industry, employment opportunities abound, and new ones are springing up every day. Just sorting through them is a major task. Where do you start?

You've already made a beginning, with the inventory process back in Chapter Two. In addition to cataloging your skills and experience, you went through exercises designed to help you pinpoint your greatest interests in life and to reveal your deepest-held dreams and ambitions. If you did your homework carefully and were honest with yourself, you probably have a clearer idea than before about the career fields that do *not* interest you, and will not have to give them a second thought. Your search area has narrowed considerably.

The next step is a trip to the reference section of a public, college, or base library—to carry your job search into a current edition of the Department of Labor's *Occupational Outlook Handbook,* a valuable source of career information for more than forty years. Updated every two years, the handbook describes in detail some 250 occupations that encompass more than 100 million jobs, or 86 percent of all the jobs our economy supports. It explains what workers actually do on the job, the training and education required, and the range of earnings to be expected. The handbook also provides summary information on another 80 occupations, covering another 5 percent of the national job total—so better than 9 out of every 10 jobs available in our economy are mentioned in its pages.

Related occupations are grouped under a dozen general headings. Here are a few examples:

> Executive, Administrative, and Managerial Occupations (accountants, analysts, and managers of all sorts)
> Professional Specialty Occupations (engineers, architects, actuaries, scientists, lawyers and judges, social and religious workers, teachers, physicians, print and electronic journalists, and performing artists)
> Technicians and Related Support Occupations (health fields, and other-than-health fields)
> Marketing and Sales Occupations (wholesale, retail, real estate, securities and financial services, travel)
> Administrative Support Occupations (adjustors, clerks and clerical supervisors, dispatchers)
> Service Occupations (protective services, food and beverage preparation, health services, personal services)
> Agriculture, Forestry, Fishing (farmers, loggers, watermen)
> Mechanics, Installers, Repairers (aircraft, autos, electronic equipment, home and farm equipment, telephones, musical instruments)
> Construction Trades (bricklayers, carpenters, electricians, plumbers, painters, roofers)
> Production Occupations (food processing, metalworking, plant and systems operators, printing, textiles, woodworking)
> Transportation and Material Moving (road, rail, water)

The handbook gets into working conditions, where the jobs are located, and projected employment trends in each field. And for each career field it also discusses related occupations that call for similar aptitudes and skills, education and training—providing a useful way of seeing whether your talents and interests have even wider application than you first imagined. Finally, the handbook provides sources of additional information: names and addresses of associations, government agencies, unions, and other organizations able to answer questions about careers. The *Occupational Outlook Handbook* is the best single source of quick career-search information—a great way to get oriented.

In the library's reference section, you also should be able to find the *Occupational Outlook Quarterly* magazine, also published by the Department of Labor. Most libraries keep several years' worth of back issues, so with any luck you can get a stack and leaf through a potpourri of careers, some conventional and some more exotic—ranging from medical illustrators to professional sports officials.

Once you have determined your short list (or even a medium-long one) of potential occupations, you can get right to work.

❯First, think of anyone you may know in each of these fields—or anyone else who may be able to pave the way for you. Write them, or better yet, call them. Tell them of your interest in their line of work and schedule some time with them to find out more about it. The chances are that they will be flattered by your seeking them out, and will be delighted to share their insights with you. Keep a record of every one of these contacts, and any follow-up contacts they may offer you. This will be the start of the networking that will become so important as your job-search effort matures. Remember—almost everyone knows someone else who may be able to help. And it may take only a single helper in the right place at the right time to boost you into the career you really want.

❯As you begin to develop your network of personal contacts and narrow your field of search, go back to the *Occupational Outlook Handbook* and check the "Sources of Additional Information" at the end of each occupational write-up. You will find anywhere from one to a half-dozen places to contact. Many of these will be associations connected with the field, and you can branch out even further with the *Encyclopedia of Associations,* also located in your library's reference section, to check out fields ranging from accounting to zoology. While you're there, let the reference librarian, who is probably linked by computer to a network of libraries, know what you're after. By training and experience, librarians are well disposed to become some of your most valuable assets in the deadly serious job-search business. Make use of their skills, and let them know how much you appreciate their help.

❯ While you are sharpening your focus on a narrowing array of possible careers, try a brainstorming drill to ensure that you are not overlooking anything. Get a copy of a local city directory or yellow pages, and start leafing through the categories of businesses, professions, goods, and services. For each new category, try to think of a concrete connection with your own life—in terms of a workplace, a worker, or a particular job—no matter how remote. Let your imagination run loose, and try to see yourself, in your mind's eye, somehow involved with each particular job category. You may trigger some interesting, even poignant, memories—and stumble across some new-career ideas that would not have popped up otherwise. In a follow-up to a recent seminar, more than half the people I asked said that they were focusing on new careers that first had appeared to them in the yellow pages!

You probably will find yourself returning to the yellow pages as your job search matures and intensifies. Let's take a hypothetical example:

Allen has had a successful military career for more than twenty years, and he is ready to retire. He has completed a personal inventory of skills and interests and learned, with no surprise, that he likes to build and direct smooth-running organizations. Allen has figured out that he is a decision maker, with well-developed leadership, organizational, and interpersonal skills. After his initial drills with the yellow pages and the occupational handbooks/

magazines, he has become interested in the health-care field. As he serves out his final preretirement winter in North Dakota, he also has decided that he never wants to pull on a set of long johns again—ever! Florida and Arizona look particularly good to him.

This is the time in your own career search to let your fingers do the walking. If your nearby library is large enough, it may have current out-of-state telephone directories; if not, send away for yellow pages that cover the cities you have targeted. You will be amazed at the number of organizations and businesses listed under health-related categories. Allen was. Here's why:

❯ The soaring costs of health care have brought about a decline in the older forms of health insurance and a dramatic rise in health-maintenance organizations, preferred-provider organizations, and physician group practices that can offer coverage to employers at a discount. Roughly 60 percent of the population is now covered by managed health-care programs (a decade ago, barely 5 percent were covered), and that percentage is virtually certain to increase, no matter what form the anticipated health-care reform eventually takes. In a few years, almost every industry in the country will be covered by some type of managed-care program. As these programs continue to proliferate, the demand for administrators, case managers, and utlization-review specialists is certain to increase. Entry-level salaries run in the thirty thousand dollar range, with top executives drawing anywhere from sixty thousand dollars to two hundred thousand dollars, although additional formal education in health administration or public health is a prerequisite for advancement.

❯ In obtaining health-care coverage for their employees, companies must assess the risk of sickness and accidents that will result in claims. Actuaries are vital to this process, ensuring that health-care companies that assume such risks are charging fair prices, while operating at a reasonable profit. In lean times, the demand for actuaries increases, because accurate predictions become more and more important and the consequences of bad predictions are felt more severely. If you have an undergraduate degree in mathematics or economics, and have the desire and ability to undergo a rigorous certification (twenty-three exams!) process, you might eventually find yourself in great demand in a durable career, where earnings range from twenty-nine thousand dollars to one hundred thousand dollars a year.

❯ Health-related sales are another growing field. The biotechnology industry, for example, is barely ten years old but is already a major force in medical technology. Biotech companies are developing—from DNA, monoclonal antibodies, and enzymes—new drugs that are more effective than synthetic drugs in attacking diseases. As more and more new products emerge from this four-billion-dollar research industry, the shortage of knowledgeable salespeople will be felt more acutely. Before the end of the century, the number of biotech researchers will probably double and the sales force in this industry should triple, at least. With a bachelor-of-science degree or equivalent and some additional technical training, you might be able to enter another long-lasting career that could lead to annual earnings in the fifty thousand to eighty-five thousand dollar range.

This is just a sampling of opportunities being created—always subject to change, of course—in a few branches of a single occupational field. Allen has a good chance of striking pay dirt.

You can see where this is going. As you warm to your own field of interest, you will probably find it useful to obtain Sunday newspapers, with their large classified advertising sections, from your target areas. This will give you an idea of employment opportunities and salary ranges, as well as other cost-of-living insights before you actually visit the area and begin contacting prospective employers. Conducting a career search at long range can be inconvenient at times, but most job hunting begins that way—and concludes successfully. That's how George and Susan did it—remember?

In looking at career fields that are most likely to remain strong through the 1990s, you will be wise to stay in touch with the nation's major concerns—e.g., health care, education, the environment, the aging population—which will absorb a large and growing share of our personnel and financial resources. By analyzing the major stories in the daily papers and weekly newsmagazines, and seeing which stories tend to lead the evening television newscasts, you can develop a generally reliable sense of what's truly important. For starters, consider this small sampling of made-to-last careers:

HEALTH

〉*Health-care design and construction.* Even while the construction industry at large (especially commercial construction) has lagged, the health-care side of it has shown steady growth at annual rates of around 5 percent. Both small, specialized firms and larger companies that want to get into the health-care business will be looking for talent.

〉*Home health care.* More than four out of five senior citizens want to remain at home in their final days, and improved technology can bring more hospital-related therapy services into the home. Employment in the home health-care field is expected to double in the next ten years or so. This means managers and administrators, as well as medical specialists.

〉*Physician's assistant, physical therapist, radiologic technologist.* Specialized jobs like these require a scientific background and rigorous training, but the demand for them will continue to increase. At present, the four thousand five hundred students trained in radiology each year have more than six thousand open positions to fill.

〉*Special-education teacher.* In most states, the law mandates that special education be made available for children who are dyslexic, emotionally disturbed, or mentally retarded, between the ages of three and twenty-one years. There is an immense and growing need for teachers in this area—a nationwide shortfall of thirty thousand or more exists at the moment. Entry-level requirements vary from state to state, with a standard teacher's certificate usually the minimum. If you have been considering a teaching career, you owe it to yourself to check out this aspect of the educational picture.

ECOLOGY AND THE ENVIRONMENT

>*Environmental engineer.* The Environmental Protection Agency has been churning out thick volumes of new regulations, and there is a need for people who can enforce them intelligently and advise companies on the best ways to comply. Massive closures of military bases will continue to pose cleanup and toxic-waste disposal problems. Colleges and universities are producing only one third of the graduates needed to fill the five thousand or so new openings each year in this field. A bachelor's degree in science or engineering is the starting point; a master's in environmental engineering is the stepping stone toward top salaries in excess of one hundred thousand dollars per year. To stay on top of this burgeoning field, contact your local reference librarian, your nearby college or university, or the Environmental Protection Agency itself.

THE AGING POPULATION

>*Mature marketing specialist.* Within twenty years, more than one third of our population will be more than fifty years old. Even today, the fifty-plus set accounts for 40 percent of total consumer demand. As the baby boomers come of age, the long-powerful youth market is deteriorating, yet relatively few mature-marketing specialists have appeared to fill the void. Check with your reference librarian to see which organizations (e.g., the Reston, Virginia-based Wolf Resources Group) sponsor training seminars in this wide-open field.

>*Travel and tourism.* Within ten years, the travel industry is expected to show more than 60 percent growth. Travel agencies and positions related to transportation systems and hotel services all will expand as this lucrative retiree market continues to grow. Inter-

ested? Ask the reference librarian for the *Encyclopedia of Associations.*

OVERSEAS OPPORTUNITIES

›*International accountant.* With foreign investment in U.S. securities and real estate exceeding the two trillion dollar mark and U.S. companies expanding their operations abroad, the demand for accountants who can provide tax, management, consulting, and auditing services for multinational clients has more than doubled since 1990. Anyone with an accounting background who has acquired foreign (area and language) expertise and can acquire additional experience in foreign business practices can move up quickly in this burgeoning field.

›*International Entrepreneur.* There is genuine hunger in both Eastern and Western Europe for joint-venture partners in selling goods and services. The timing has never been better. Many U.S. universities offer entrepreneur classes for would-be small business owners and overseas investors. The market is wide open.

A NEW PAIR OF GLASSES

New avenues to successful, interest-driven careers are opening every day, even as the number of more traditional jobs continues to shrink. The trick is to make the magic connection between your own situation and the new opportunities.

Think about the ways you gather information each day: from newspapers and magazines, radio and television, conversation with others, and just plain observation of life around you. Actually, there's not much "gathering" at all. We are bombarded with information, and the only way to keep ourselves from becoming saturated with it each day is to screen much of it out, either consciously or subconsciously.

Writers and editors know this, and they present most news stories in classic inverted-pyramid style, setting out the most compelling facts and observations in the headline and lead paragraph and moving through the story with information of descending importance. That way, the story can be cut from the bottom to fit available space, and the reader can break off when his curiosity has been satisfied.

The information keeps flowing past us, but relatively little of it gets processed. We tend to skim through reading material and tune out much of what is broadcast each day. We almost have to. Otherwise, we would be supersaturated with information before lunchtime. The down side of this, however, is that some helpful career-search information passes through unheeded.

To preclude such leakage of valuable information, keep in mind that opportunities often come disguised as problems, and that in your years of military service you have solved a lot of them, ranging from low morale and base beautification to survival under extremes of weather, climate, or danger. A problem-solving mind set is quite likely one of your strengths.

As the armed forces do, CivLand has plenty of problems. The news, both broadcast and print, is filled with them every day— often concentrated in areas of mounting national interest: health care, the environment, changes in requirements of an aging population (housing, transportation, marketing, etc.), and interest in world trade and overseas markets. Recently, I looked through four Sunday newspapers from medium-size cities in Connecticut, Virginia, Michigan, and Tennessee. Each had more than twenty (one had thirty-four) articles centered on these seven major concerns, which—from our new pespective—can be seen as needs that could be filled in one way or another.

As a potential problem solver, you might look at such stories in the following way:

> Just what *is* the problem being described?
> Is anyone doing anything about it?
> If not, why not?
> If solutions were tried in the past, why did they fail?

> What is your solution? Write it down, trying to be as specific as possible. The devil is in the details.
> Can you tackle this problem by yourself in the short term, or will you require more time, more research, and outside assistance?
> Finally, how much do you want to take on such a project?

Let's look at two examples—one rather basic and straightforward, the other more complex and time-consuming:

A young woman in St. Louis was a regular patron of her neighborhood laundromat. After a while, she became conscious of the fact that harried mothers seemed to be spending half their time wrestling with the laundry and an equal amount of time trying to keep their young children under control. She suggested to the owner that he put in some durable toys and child-size tables, and perhaps a television set tuned to kiddie shows—the perfect pacifier. The owner complied, the word got out, and more young mothers began to show up at this laundromat, which catered more to their needs than the others. The next step was to install a television set for the mothers, so they could watch the daytime game shows and soap operas during the long wash and dry cycles. More and more customers were coming, and staying longer, so she encouraged the owner to set up some food and beverage vending machines, and arranged for a nearby delicatessen to take orders in the laundromat. After a while, the young woman with all the ideas learned that some steady customers had problems getting their laundry done during periods of foul weather, so she arranged for a minivan to pick them up and take them home. At this point, the owner enlarged his laundromat to handle the increased demand, and asked the innovative young woman to become his business partner. They soon opened another laundromat in another part of town, complete with baby-sitting facilities, television, food, and transportation. At last count, they were getting ready to open their fifth laundromat.

In Connecticut, a New Haven resident saw a problem in a 1986 newspaper article—and thought of a potential solution. Rush-hour driving conditions along Interstate 95 were becoming so crowded that the situation would soon become unmanageable unless new lanes were constructed at a cost of billions. An AMTRAK railroad line ran parallel to I-95 between New Haven and Boston, and this would-be entrepreneur came up with the idea of establishing morning and evening commuter service along the existing track, at a fraction of the projected road-building cost. In 1990, the Shore Line Railroad, using rebuilt engines and old passenger cars that had been refurbished, was up and running—taking hundreds of cars off the highway, cutting down pollution from auto exhausts, and saving commuters a great deal of time and money. But first, the concept had to be sold to the Connecticut Department of Transportation, then to the state's governor. Research was needed into the costs of refurbishing old equipment, leasing the AMTRAK rails, setting up and operating commuter stations, and manning the system, which grew to include bus transportation for commuters in New Haven. Once determined, these costs and start-up times had to be compared with highway-construction estimates for the wisdom of the concept to be validated. Many other commuter rail systems and feeder airlines have similar stories to tell.

If the jump from laundromat to railroad line seems a bit much to you, let's look at something in between. Today, a significant trend in the bookselling industry is toward "super stores" (Barnes & Noble have opened a hundred of them since 1990). But another New Haven entrepreneur had a different vision and opened a combination bookstore/cafe near the Yale University campus some years ago. He served coffee, soups, salads, and desserts to the browsers, many of whom became regular customers. The concept caught on, and he now operates four such places. The cafe part of each is profitable enough to operate independently, and the book sales are better than average.

Sometimes, a chance remark can turn on that creative light switch in your head. Take the case of Janet, a Coast Guard petty officer who decided to retire in her home town of Monroe, Louisiana. Knowing that opportunities were limited, she started looking through a copy of the Monroe yellow pages, and began asking friends back home about goods and services that were currently in demand there. Something clicked during a telephone conversation with her sister, who said, "I'd like to return to the work force myself, but I just can't find a good sitter for my kids." Janet went back to the yellow pages, and found only two day-care centers listed there. She checked further, and found that both centers were operating at full capacity and had long waiting lists for new customers.

With a year and a half to go until retirement, Janet enrolled in a course in early childhood education at a community college near her Coast Guard duty station. On weekends and during leave periods, she worked at a day-care center, gaining practical experience while validating something she always had sensed about herself: She could be a very patient person, and she really did like to be around kids. Her Coast Guard experience had left her with a good eye for detail and a strong sense of organization. She was confident that she possessed a winning combination of attributes for her chosen line of work, and managed to convince the owner of one of Monroe's two centers. Together, they opened a third center to be managed by Janet, and they since have become partners in yet a fourth center, meeting a strong local demand for child care that had existed for quite some time.

5

THE RÉSUMÉ:
A FOOT IN THE DOOR

Y ou have narrowed your career choices and targeted your potential employers. But you can't just start knocking on doors and asking for work. First, you must get an interview with someone who can hire you. And to get an interview, you will need an introduction—a written introduction.

Let's get one thing clear at the outset: by itself, even the best résumé in the world will not get you a job. You might be able to create a life history of wisdom, strength, and virtue, but at best you will be admired from afar, without a single job offer to show for it. No firm is going to hire someone solely on the basis of a piece of paper—one provided by the applicant, at that.

If you do things correctly, however, your résumé will jump out of the stack of papers that the hiring firm's initial screener (in the personnel office) must wade through—and it will find its way to the desk of a recruiter, or the personnel director, or even a vice-president, perhaps. If the résumé and its cover letter do the job, the senior executive will see a matchup of the company's needs with the skills and experience you will bring to the firm. Only then will the executive call for an interview, to check things out.

So the typical résumé writer is in a position similar to Zsa Zsa Gabor's newest husband. He has a fair idea of what is expected; the real trick is to make it interesting, because most résumés are deadly dull. I know—I have read thousands during my recruiting experience, sometimes more than one hundred a day for some of the larger firms. I have yet to meet a recruiter or a personnel manager who actually enjoys reading a stack of résumés. The very thought makes my eyes glaze over—and I am not alone, as a recent survey shows: Only six of every hundred résumés gets past the initial screener, who spends an average of only fifteen to thirty seconds per paper on the first high-speed scan. That half minute— at most—is not much time to dazzle an experienced, deadline-fighting screener with a quick trigger finger, who has been instructed to send forward only the résumés that promise something useful to the firm.

So how do you survive the initial scan—over so many competitors? Helpful advice abounds. On my most recent trip to the New York public library, I counted more than 110 books that deal with résumé writing. If you want to read them all, go ahead. But there is a less cumbersome way to come up with that attention-grabbing résumé. I'll give you some good news up front: If you have done the self-analysis homework called for in the second chapter, you may already be more than two thirds of the way through the soul-searching needed to put together a decent résumé.

TRAPS TO AVOID

Before we get started, let's look at the down side for a moment, to see some of the traps you must avoid in selling your talent and experience to an employer who can afford to be selective. Here is a list of résumé killers, as seen by recruiters and employers across the nation.

❯*Poor reproduction.* We've already established that the readers are hard-pressed for time. What do you think they will do with illegible or barely legible résumés?

❯*Lack of graphic appeal.* The type is legible, but the résumé is four pages long, single spaced, with no margins—like a crank letter. The same turnoff occurs when a one-page résumé is puffed to two or more pages, through excessive use of white space.

>*Poor spelling; typographical errors; poor grammar.* Any of these is the kiss of death.

>*Overwritten; saying little of value.* "I was born at an early age under the sign of . . . "

>*Little real information.* Just dates and titles of positions held. Lists of duties, not accomplishments. Not results oriented.

>*Irrelevant material.* Your physical dimensions, civic activities, noble causes, and hobbies are of no interest to recruiters unless they have a direct bearing on the job you are seeking. Even worse is a gratuitous attempt to make a virtue of necessity through a ringing assertion of good health. This tends to irritate résumé readers, who feel that for any applicant good health should go without saying. The same goes for a statement that references will be provided on request. If you *don't* have references, you have some tall explaining to do.

>*Distortions.* There is a not-so-fine line between stating your experience and qualifications in a favorable way and deliberately misleading the résumé reader. Remember, a résumé is a means to an end. The real key to a job offer is the interview, if your résumé can set one up. You will not walk into the interview with a clean slate. It will be partially covered by your résumé's claims, and the interviewer will set about filling the blanks with the persistence of an investigative journalist. Don't set yourself up for the horrible embarrassment of seeing your credibility unraveled—and your job prospects in that industry shattered (bad news travels quickly)—by a tenacious line of questioning, once the interviewer's suspicions are aroused.

>*Bizarre packaging.* I have polled many recruiters and personnel directors, and about 95 percent of them agree that gimmicks may gain some attention but rarely lead to interviews. The other 5 percent I polled came from creative professions—e.g., advertising, marketing, public relations—where résumés with a flair tend to fare better. Just remember—you must live up to whatever early excitement you create when you enter the interview room later on. A

recruiter for J. Walter Thompson, one of the world's largest advertising agencies, once stated that most purveyors of unusual résumés fall flat at interview time. When they are challenged to produce some steak to go with the sizzle, they can't.

BUILDING THE RIGHT RÉSUMÉ

There are three basic types of résumés: *Chronological, Functional,* and *Targeted.* Each will have strong points and weak points, in your particular case. Let's take a look at them:

❯*Chronological.* This starts with your most recent duty assignment or job experience and works back toward your earliest, following the path you took in the self-analysis of your military experience. If you have had a tightly focused military career with assignments of increasing responsibility (e.g., in the supply or data-processing fields)—especially if your preretirement assignment is a natural stepping stone into the civilian position you seek—the chronological approach may be best. You can highlight your strengths, your achievements, and your potential value to the hiring company. Recruiters and other résumé readers like the chronological approach, too, because they can make their own assessments of your career path—how demanding your assignments were and how frequently you received special recognition and promotions. They also will be alert to any gaps or apparent omissions in the chronology—and will mark them as areas for the interviewers to probe. Their ultimate objective is to determine, in terms of their own experience with thousands of résumés and their knowledge of the firm and the industry, whether a valid matchup with the person portrayed in the résumé seems to exist. After a while, they get pretty good at it.

Most military retirees, however, are not specialists. They have taken generalist career paths, in which strong performance in a wide range of assignments is seen as the best route to high-level command and other positions of authority. Such breadth of experience may outweigh more detailed knowledge in a narrow field, but this point is difficult to make in a chronological format. We need another type of résumé:

> *Functional.* This organizes information under functional or topical headings, such as Supervision, Recruiting, Project Management, or Teaching. Each paragraph covers a single category with statements related to your own experiences in it. After you have narrowed your selection of potential career fields, you can achieve the greatest impact by listing functions in descending order of importance to the field you seek. Feel free to create new functional headings to showcase your strengths—e.g., "Innovative Talents," to show how you have solved problems in unusual or creative ways throughout your career. I like a functional résumé, because it lets you bring out the substance of your career—rather than recite a string of military titles that may be unfamiliar to recruiters and other résumé readers.

On the other hand, many readers view functional résumés with near-pathological unhappiness, because they are harder to fathom. Instead of a clear look at an orderly progression of career assignments, they often see a smorgasbord of self-serving comments—nearly impossible to place into context. There are no weaknesses evident anywhere. Most recruiters know better.

If you decide to prepare a functional résumé, you can allay some of this suspicion by avoiding grandiose phrases ("significantly enhanced unit combat readiness") that sound as though they were pulled from award citations. Instead—after referring to your notes from the Chapter Two exercise—get specific, using numbers whenever you can ("reduced 'down time' of battalion vehicles awaiting maintenance by fourteen percent over an eighteen-month period"). Along that line, if you have supervised or managed people, say how many. If you have had budget responsibility, say how much.

If you make quantifiable claims, be ready to have them checked out. Many companies are meticulous about this. If you write a teaser like "Reorganized the public-affairs office to permit more creative use of part-time civilian workers; increased efficiency and reduced costs,'' the interviewers may invite you to give dollar amounts and tell them just how you pulled it off. Be prepared to provide details.

To write a functional résumé, you need to have the requirements of a specific career field (or two, or three) firmly in mind, so you can tailor your functional areas to those requirements. But you might be able to go beyond that, if you have a clear notion of a particular position that has attracted your interest. Instead of a career in municipal government, for instance, you may have decided to try for the vacant post of the city manager of Centerville. In such a case, additional résumé tailoring is in order:

➤ *Targeted*. The targeted resume, zooming in on a specific job, is the easiest to write, and the easiest for the recruiters to understand. It should include the following zones of information:

* *Job target*. A description of the job you are seeking, specific enough to attract the attention of the official in the firm who is responsible for that activity.

* *Capabilities*. This should show work that you are *capable* of performing, even though you may not have done it before. You can stress your qualifications here without being held hostage by your own work history.

* *Accomplishments*. Here is the place to cite the things you have *actually done* that are related to the position you seek. In this connection, I always look for evidence that you have trained and developed your subordinates, to make them eligible for promotion. This is particularly important in smaller companies, where you will be expected to wear many hats. A hands-on manager who gets involved in the advancement of his juniors is always welcome— and a prerequisite for that manager's own promotion often is the need to groom a replacement.

* *Miscellaneous*. This is a summary of your pertinent work history, education, and other qualifications, e.g., language skills: ''Fluent in Japanese,'' or ''Fluent in French, with a working knowledge of Spanish and German.'' Familiarity with other cultures also is

critical in this shrinking world (''Served as naval attaché in Athens; strong knowledge of language, culture, and protocol.'').

In developing the targeted résumé, you need to acquire as much information as you can about the skills required for the position you target. The best source is the horse's mouth—the incumbent or someone close by—if you can acquire that sort of privileged information in a discreet way. But you must be careful in evaluating both the quality of the information and the source—the latest rumor from just anyone who happens to work there usually won't do.

Because it is important to define the targeted position accurately, and in a way that will dovetail well with your capabilities and accomplishments, feel free to rewrite the job-target portion as often as needed, to get it just right. It is the linchpin of the targeted résumé.

As you move into the ''capabilities'' zone, take a separate sheet of scratch paper and think of the best ''can do'' talent or skill you can bring to the job you've just described in such careful detail. Then think of another talent, and keep going until you run out of linkages between the demands of the job and your bag of attributes. With any luck, there will be at least a dozen (if you run dry quickly, you might ponder whether you are applying for the right job). Then pare this list down to the best six or eight action-oriented statements in descending order of importance (combining some, if appropriate) about your qualifications for this particular position.

On a separate sheet of paper, start listing your accomplishments—both in and outside of military service—that relate to this position. Earlier, in preparing more general résumés, I advised you not to list civic activities and other outside interests, because most of them were irrelevant. But in this more-focused, targeted résumé, certain aspects of outside activities can help you make your case. For example, being a member of the local Civitan club says little in itself; on the other hand, running a successful charity drive, or publishing an award-winning newsletter, or leading a productive membership campaign for Civitan will go far to bolster your claims of accomplishment in organizing, communicating, or recruiting.

Once again, list every pertinent accomplishment you can, then boil the list down to six or eight of the best, combining accomplishments where feasible.

Your final scratch sheet, summarizing your work history and education, is more of a routine listing, but you still should arrange things to highlight your suitability for the targeted position, in the best way possible.

You are now ready to "go smooth," with a concise description of the job you want and three tightly packed zones of backup material that show clearly your fitness for that particular position. All this should fit on a single page—or two, at most. Almost everyone prefers one page, but two out of three recruiters say that they will hold still for two pagers. Just be sure your strongest points are made on the first page! [NOTE: Here's the exception that proves the rule: If you have extensive training or education in your targeted field, or have written extensively about it, or have received a number of awards for accomplishment in that field, list them on a separate page and attach it to the résumé. Especially valuable is any evidence that your accomplishments have come under difficult conditions. A hiring authority for a troubled firm might decide that your record of success in adverse situations may provide the key to a solution for them.]

I am a big fan of targeted résumés. They go straight to the point, saving your time and the recruiter's. If you are truly suited for the job you want, a résumé that says so directly will outshine a more generalized one every time. As you begin your job search, uncertain about your ultimate career field, you must rely upon a more general résumé, either chronological or functional. But as you narrow the search, you may wish to fine-tune your general résumé, to focus on two or three promising leads. Eventually, the time will arrive for you to prepare a clean-cut, concise, targeted résumé. At this stage, you should be able to target several jobs simultaneously—with full confidence—making slight adjustments in each new résumé as needed.

OTHER THINGS TO THINK ABOUT

We've been through some glaring mistakes that can kill a résumé in its infancy. It's time to look at more subtle aspects of résumé writing that also can turn into show stoppers:

❯*The Objective.* By and large, you are better off placing a brief job or career objective on your résumé and in your cover letter. Many employers read those résumés before any others, and in large firms a statement of the objective can assist in routing the résumé from the initial screener to the appropriate department for further review. Unfortunately, about half of the statements read something like:

> Seeking a challenging career in a progressive company which will provide me opportunity for growth in a stimulating environment which will enable me to use my skills and experience to contribute to the growth and success of the company.

Well, who *wouldn't* want all that?

I detest time-wasting statements like that one. And so do most other résumé readers. Saying absolutely nothing, such statements waste our time and insult our intelligence. One paragraph like that is almost certain to kill the rest of the résumé, no matter how carefully it's been crafted—*if* anyone bothers to read the rest of the résumé.

Keep your objective statement short and to the point:

"Seeking job opportunity in personnel recruiting."
or
"Seeking career opportunity in benefits administration."

—and let it work *for* you, not against you.

❯*The age thing.* It is illegal to discriminate against employees or applicants because of their ages. And it is well known that older workers often prove to be generally more reliable, and often better choices for employment. Nevertheless, it is also well known that many companies have their own informal policies that do not favor applicants more than forty years old. If you are uncertain about a company's or an industry's attitude, don't lead with your chin by volunteering your college or high school graduation dates. Many screeners are quite adept at subtracting twenty-one or seventeen years, as the case may be, to calculate your birth year. Once in the interview room, you will get your chance to go around the firm's preconceptions about age—with a display of drive and vigor, in addition to your impressive bearing.

❯*Have briefcase, will travel.* If you are mobile, say so ("Willing to travel extensively and relocate; prefer the Northwest" or "Will travel or relocate throughout the United States and overseas"). Mobility usually makes you more employable.

❯*Demilitarize for clarity.* For more than a few years, while the Vietnam syndrome was operating full blast, the conventional wisdom for job seekers was to write résumés so opaque that reviewers could never tell if they'd seen even one day of military service. For instance, a job description for an advisor to the South Vietnamese Marine Corps (who blew up a key bridge and stalled the 1972 North Vietnamese Easter offensive) might have read:

> Consultant to multibillion-dollar international agency, with dynamic, hands-on experience in transportation systems; mechanical, electrical, and civil engineering; telecommunications networks; short-, medium-, and long-range strategies; and competitive inventory-reduction techniques.

Who is kidding whom?

With the armed forces now listed among the nation's most-admired institutions, that sort of silliness is long gone. But the presence of military jargon in your résumé can still confuse a civilian reader, and also can leave the impression that you are not quite ready to let go of your first career. For example, words like "commanded" could well be changed to the civilian near equivalents "directed," "administered," "coordinated," or the like. "Combat" could be translated as "extremely hazardous conditions," and "combat-ready troops" could emerge as "highly trained personnel." You get the drift. If in doubt, get a friend from CivLand to check out your résumé for readability.

❯*The draft dodge.* If you provide a rough draft of your résumé to business contacts for their constructive criticism, use the occasion to ask where it might be sent for best effect. This can gain you some solid résumé-writing advice plus a step forward in networking with new contacts.

Sometimes, the circulation of a draft résumé produces some spectacular results. A Coast Guard chief petty officer stationed in New Haven, Connecticut, gave his first draft to four civilian neighbors. A week later, one neighbor called him and said, "I've talked to my two partners, and we'd like to talk to you. We may have a position for you."

The chief was flabbergasted. "You don't know me that well, and I don't even know what kind of business you're in. Why would you want to hire me?"

"You have a background in running an office staff and seem to have a good working knowledge of computers and office automation. Our small firm—forty employees—is growing. The three of us devote most of our time to the operations side of our metal-coating plant. We need someone to organize the office staff and upgrade our information systems."

Up to that point, the chief had been thinking about retirement in the Southwest, but the partners won him over. He took the job, performed well, and after two years received a piece of the partnership.

❯*No time for weirdness.* Earlier, I warned against producing bizarre résumés. In addition to provocative wording, the packaging and means of delivery have often gone to extreme lengths of creativity, as shown by these real examples:

* One firm received a potted plant, a résumé, and a note, saying "My growth has been remarkable, too."

* Other résumés have been delivered in pizza boxes—or by belly dancers.

* A Chicago recruiter received by messenger the arm and leg of a mannequin, with a résumé and a note: "I'd give an arm and a leg for that marketing job!"

* The chief pilot for a major Southwest firm received a résumé by telegram, asking him to look skyward at 2:00 P.M. on a certain day. There, in skywriting, he saw "Hire Me!"—and the applicant's initials.

Do these tactics get attention? You bet they do. Do they lead to interviews? Rarely. Recruiters tend to see a resort to gimmicks as a way of camouflaging lack of substance.

What works best? A resume that *you* have written about yourself. If you really want to, you can hire a professional résumé-writing service for anywhere from fifty dollars to five hundred dollars, and you will get a document free of rough spots. It also will be devoid of recognizable material about *you*—and will probably appear that way to other readers, as well. The price probably will include a hundred or more printed copies, with binders that also identify the résumé as a glossy professional product. The only way you get your money's worth from that deal is to come up with a hundred dry holes. If you decide to change your résumé, say, by moving to a targeted one, you are stuck with a lot of I-love-me sheets, nicely bound.

On the other hand, if you write the résumé yourself (letting a few friends give it a sanity check), and use a letter-quality computer printer or business typewriter to put it on quality bond paper (white, off-white, buff, or gray) in black ink, you will have a thoroughly professional and personal product. This way, you can adjust your résumé easily, reproducing only as many copies as you need until you print the one that lands you the job-clinching interview.

But don't quit then. A résumé is never complete. As you continue to develop new skills and add new work experience, *write it down,* then file it. You never can tell when another opportunity will beckon, and you'll want to update your résumé.

DON'T FORGET THE COVER LETTER

The key to gaining the competitive edge is getting your résumé into the right hands. Conversely, the quickest way to get your résumé lost in the shuffle is to send it in without a cover letter. Believe me—a résumé out of the blue commands no special attention. It is treated like a real ho hummer, *even though the recipient may have requested it.* How could that be? It's easy to explain. I've been there myself.

After meeting someone at a luncheon or dinner, I would get into a conversation about job opportunities and wind up suggesting that the individual send a résumé to me or to another recruiter. Some time later, an unadorned résumé would cross my desk. If neither too much time nor too many résumés had intervened, I *might* have made the connection without prompting. On the other hand, if the résumé came in late or at the suggestion of another recruiter (without that fact being made clear), its chances for special handling were just about nil.

Don't let this happen to you! All you need is a short letter—no more than one page, ever. Here are a few things to consider:

❯*The heading and salutation.* Always try to address the recipient by name (double-check the spelling), whenever possible. If you are responding to an ad that lists no one by name, call the company. If you still cannot get a name, avoid the stilted "To whom it may concern" and the less-stilted but still-tedious "Dear sir or madam." Try an upbeat "Good morning!" instead.

❯*The body.* You need to explain why you are writing (why you are interested in the company) and what you have to offer (why the company should be interested in you). Try to get off to a fast start:

> *Dear Fred,*
>   *I am really excited about the job opportunities you mentioned at the Rotary Club dinner last evening . . .*

or

> *Bud Taylor at Stanley Products said you are looking for*
> *a new regional sales manager and suggested that I send*
> *you my résumé . . .*

or

> *Your ad in this morning's* Times *really caught my atten-*
> *tion . . .*

Next, state briefly why the hiring firm should be interested in you:

> *In a similar situation, while in charge of a Midwestern*
> *recruiting station, I reorganized the territory and was*
> *consistently ten to fifteen percent over quota for three*
> *years . . .*

> *The Closing.* Your final comment should promise a follow through:

> *Would you be available for a meeting within two weeks,*
> *to discuss ways I might be of benefit to Mohawk Alumi-*
> *num, Inc.? I'll call Monday, and attempt to arrange a*
> *mutually convenient meeting date.*

Keep it short, giving the reader some reasons both to read your résumé carefully and to continue the dialogue face to face.

The appearance of your cover letter is vital. It shows whether you are capable of paying proper attention to a most important matter. You wouldn't throw on a warm-up jacket over formal wear, so please don't cover your attractive résumé with a form letter or copy paper. Use the same quality and color paper as your résumé's, with the same letter-quality printing in black ink. Letterhead stationery—nothing fancy, just first name, middle initial, and last name at the top of the page—adds a nice touch. Be sure that the letter is centered and balanced on the page, with short paragraphs for quick skimming and reading. Have friends look it over, as they did your résumé. Double-check for spelling and typos, as well as any grammatical glitches.

You have spent a lot of time and effort on your résumé; yet the cover letter, usually written more in haste, often makes a greater first impression. Don't let that little one pager pull the rug from under you!

Finally, don't forget to sign the cover letter. You'd be amazed at how many forget, pegging themselves as inattentive to detail.

THE THIRD-PARTY LETTER

The most effective cover letter often comes from an interested third party, who can toot *your* horn without reservation or fear of embarrassment:

> *Dear Fred:*
>
> *Enclosed is the résumé of Peter Austin, whom I met at a Lions Club dinner last week. He will be leaving the Marine Corps within the next six months.*
>
> *Peter is leaning toward a career in advertising.*
>
> *He is bright, articulate, personable, and well motivated.*
>
> *He is a very interesting and capable guy—well worth meeting.*
>
> *All best,*

A FINAL THOUGHT

The résumé reader is less concerned about helping you meet your career objectives than about helping the firm meet *its* objectives—with the help of you or someone else. In laying out your talents and skills in your résumé and cover letter, you must cause this tantalizing thought to flash through the reader's mind:

"Hey—this guy can help us!"

The following cover letter and résumé samples are provided for general guidance only. Feel free to make adjustments in format and writing style, if they fit your own situation better.

Figure 4. Sample Cover Letter

1074 Greene Drive
Salem, Oregon 97224
(503) 555–1918
February 2, 1994

Mr. William H. Cook
City Administrator
P.O. Box 950
McMinnville, Oregon 97128

Dear Mr. Cook,
I have read of your need for an assistant city administrator, and I am interested in the position. The enclosed résumé will substantiate the highlights of my career in the U.S. Navy:

- Developed and demonstrated strong leadership ability, along with trouble-shooting and organizational skills
- Compiled consistent track record of increasing productivity while reducing costs
- Reorganized and consolidated major engineering and recreational programs
- Directed "with distinction" a formal engineering school with 26 courses, 250 instructors, and 4,500 students.

I look back with pride on a highly successful naval career and look forward to an equally challenging and enjoyable career in the civilian sector. My date of retirement from the Navy is still flexible.

I will call you between 10:00 A.M. and noon on Monday, February 14, to discuss this opening further. I am eager to see if my experience and abilities can benefit McMinnville.

Sincerely,

John L. Campbell

Figure 5. Chronological Résumé

Peter B. Cunningham
28 Kilburn Road
Fairfax, Virginia 22030
Office: (703) 555–5541
Home: (703) 555–2828

Summary:
- Clear communicator, oral and written.
- Hands-on leadership; a team player.
- Proven problem solver.
- Extensive experience in successfully managing and coordinating diverse programs involving training, administration, budgetary planning, public relations, and counseling.

1990–Present: **Deputy Director, Personnel—Washington, D.C.**
Managed a mixed civilian and military personnel work force of about 470 at national headquarters level. Functional areas included assignment, performance rating, promotion, retention, separation, and retirement.

1987–1990: **Director, Recruit Training—San Diego, California**
Responsible for processing, orientation, and training of twenty-five thousand recruits annually. Supervised a staff of more than five hundred officers and drill instructors. Made more than fifty public-speaking appearances, including television and radio talk shows.

1985–1987: **Director of Operations, Expeditionary Brigade—Oahu, Hawaiian Islands**
Developed operational orders and plans for a wide range of possible contingencies in the Indian Ocean, Persian Gulf, and Western Pacific. Directed and coordinated complex combat-training exercises for organization of three thousand—often with units of other nations and other U.S. forces—which required extensive verbal and written communications skills and powers of observation, analysis, and flexibility.

1983–1985: **Commanding Officer, Infantry Battalion—Oahu**
Directed a combat organization of one thousand with responsibilities encompassing training, planning, budgeting and financial management, and personnel administration and counseling in family and financial matters, job performance, and career development.

1980–1983: **Director of Recruiting—Nashville, Tennessee**
Managed a recruiting force of 150 civilian and military workers in twenty-four offices covering three states. Responsibilities included extensive public speaking to sell the benefits and opportunities of military service, organizing and training recruiting-station staffs, and budget planning. Unfailingly met or exceeded sales quotas, with high percentage of recruits successfully completing difficult entry-level training.

1965–1980: **Wide Range of Assignments, Including:**
- Tour as instructor, NROTC Unit, Duke University, Durham, North Carolina.
- Command assignments at rifle platoon and rifle company level.
- Staff assignments in operations, logistics, and intelligence fields.
- Completion of four formal military schools.

Education: **Florida State University—Tallahassee, Florida (B.A., History)**

Figure 6. Functional Résumé

John L. Campbell
1074 Greene Drive
Salem, Oregon 97224
(503) 555–1918

Objective   A career in city and municipal management

Career History   More than twenty-eight years experience in positions of
increasing responsibility. Hands-on, in-depth experience in
civil engineering, planning and project management, administrative and personnel services, resources management,
and training.

Organizational   In the U.S. Navy, managed resources and equipment and
Management   supervised from 250 to 1,500 construction personnel in nu-
merous horizontal and vertical construction projects, in the
United States and overseas. Developed work element, material, equipment and manpower estimates. Prepared work
schedules and project progress reports. Designed specific
projects, performed required surveying, and used critical-
path method of planning, scheduling, and control.

Planned and completed the reorganization and consolida-
tion of five operational engineer units into a single organization. Increased productivity by 25 percent and equipment
availability by 40 percent in first eight months.

Reorganized and consolidated athletic and recreational programs of seven major commands, with assets in excess of
one hundred million dollars. Reduced operating costs by 20
percent and property losses by 80 percent, while increasing
program effectiveness by 30 percent during the first year
of operation.

Budgeting and   Planned nine cyclic budget submissions for Congressional
Program   hearings. Prepared procurement plans with an average fund-
Management   ing level of twenty million dollars per year.

Data Processing/ Systems Analysis

Developed computerized civil engineering support plan to identify new construction requirements. Reduced response time by 80 percent and increased reliability by 75 percent in pinpointing personnel and material requirements to support military operations.

Training Management/ Administration

Director/chief executive officer of formal school providing twenty-six courses at basic through supervisory levels. Reduced student failure rate from eight percent to less than one percent in two years. Gained accreditation for all courses offered.

Logistics, Maintenance, Transportation Management

Managed air, sea, and land transportation requirements of naval forces in the Western Pacific. Assisted in development of the agreements with three foreign governments that covered host-nation support for U.S. forces stationed in their countries.

Education

Master of Science (International Affairs)
    The George Washington University
Bachelor of Science (Civil Engineering)
    Virginia Polytechnic Institute
U.S. Naval War College (Command and Staff)
    [Postgraduate midlevel management course]
U.S. National War College
    [Postgraduate top-level management course]
Defense Language Institute
    [Working knowledge of Italian]

Figure 7. Targeted Résumé

Larry D. Harbison
108 Memory Lane
Fayetteville, North Carolina 28644
(919) 555–0242

Job Target: Research assistant with urban/regional planning firm capabilities:

- Write complete and detailed research reports.
- Edit written materials for content and grammar.
- Work long hours without physical or emotional stress.
- Communicate effectively with librarians, engineers, and others who support research work.
- Read and summarize detailed and complex reference works.
- Plan and carry out complicated tasks.
- Sketch and draw charts and other visuals to supplement descriptive text.

Achievements: • Served as assistant editor of military base newspaper; wrote articles about military and social issues.
- Conducted research to develop training manual.
- Wrote prizewinning essay on crime in urban settings.
- Was editor of high school yearbook.

Work History: 1979–present, U.S. Army (Sergeant First Class)

Education: Anne Arundel Community College, Arnold, Maryland (Associate of Arts)

6

....

GETTING THE INTERVIEW: HOW TO OPEN THE DOOR

Even a successful job campaign can be the pits—it really can. You can suffer enough rejection to shake your self-assurance to its foundations. Your self-discipline, patience, endurance, and creativity will be tested to the extreme. If you do not have quick success, you may discover new depths of despair. An Air Force wife once told me that the transition was pure hell for her husband, comparable only to childbirth itself.

Must it always be that way? Not at all. For many, the job search has been an exciting experience in exploring new worlds—reaching for the stars that have marked their lifelong ambitions.

What makes the difference? First, it is doing your homework, to prepare yourself to make intelligent choices and perform well under scrutiny. Then, it means believing with all your heart that somewhere out there is a job—and a career—with your name on it.

You need to carry two basic attitudes into the job search:

❯*Your ability to obtain good interviews will be limited only by your own perseverance and creativity.* A Marine once told me that he never realized how persistent and creative he had to become in developing bits of information into solid leads and strong opportunities. His own search led to two career fields, with three or four solid opportunities emerging in each field. But it took time and patience for him to develop his network of contacts. This leads us to the other basic attitude:

❭*Laugh a lot.* Take your work seriously, but don't take yourself too seriously. The Laws of Murphy virtually guarantee that some dumb things will happen to you along the way: If they *can* happen, they *will*. All you can do is take your hits, shake them off, and move on toward your goal. Your ability to make the best of an awkward situation will work in your favor.

Here's an example: Some years ago, while working as a recruiter, I sent a highly qualified candidate to interview with a client in Kansas City. On his way into the office, he tripped in the doorway and went sprawling in a perfect three-point landing in front of the client.

As soon as possible after the interview, the candidate sent the employer a letter by express mail, under a letterhead he had created for the purpose:

Ringling Bros., Barnum & Bailey Circus

Dear Mr. Cooper,

We are always on the lookout for new talent. I under-stand that you have just interviewed a young man whose promising skills as a marketing manager may be eclipsed by his slapstick talent as a clown, during and after duty hours. If you are unable to use him, please send him to us.

/s/P. T. Barnum

The employer really liked the young man's ability to laugh at himself and regroup quickly after an evident disaster. So he made him an offer for the marketing manager's position.

This is not to suggest that you give the Laws of Murphy a nudge and create your own disasters, in order to demonstrate your bounce-back skills. But if you never lose hope, there's always a chance to turn misfortune around.

KEEP A RECORD

We'll be discussing the most-used ways to obtain interviews, and others that are less conventional. But first, you should prepare to keep a diary—a permanent record of contacts and important data you will collect in the course of your search. A small loose-leaf notebook, something that will fit into a briefcase, is ideal for this. Once you enter the transition business, that notebook will become your constant companion. Don't even think of leaving home without it!

You need a handy, permanent job-search record for two reasons:

❯If you are going to leave no stone unturned, you will need checklists and memory joggers. A truly thorough job search will turn up new leads at the most unexpected times, and you cannot rely solely on your memory for prompt attention and followup.

❯If the averages hold true, you could be back in the job market within two to five years. Why start all over again? If you have your job-search file handy, you can update it with new contacts, new industry developments, and potential job opportunities—and get back into the game all the more quickly.

THE MAIN ROUTES TO EMPLOYMENT

Mark the first section of your job-search notebook with a tab labeled "Main Routes." These are the most obvious sources of employment information, which will give you your first snapshot of the prospects in your chosen field(s). You can log in any leads you develop—along with action taken, action still pending, and pertinent dates.

Let's take a look at some of these main routes, and their pros and cons:

❯*Newspapers.* Building upon your earlier work with telephone books and city directories, start reading the business section and the classified and display ads of the local papers, for a general feeling of movement in your chosen field(s). If you are interested in settling in a distant metropolitan area, you can use the out-of-town newspaper section of your nearest library. For papers from smaller towns, you may have to rely upon friends or relatives—or spring for a subscription or two yourself, once you have focused your search.

❯*Employment Agencies.* They are not really interested in you unless you are available immediately (or at worst, within thirty days). You generally will do better with them if you have a marketable—preferably technical—skill. Many agencies specialize in a limited number of fields. Ask if they cover your area(s) of interest. If not, move on. They will not be your best bet, even though their fee is almost always paid by the hiring companies.

❯*Executive Search Firms.* They get paid retainers by client companies to find specific individuals to fill specific openings. Your résumé goes into their files, and will get a future look only when it matches up with one of their search missions. Again—don't hold your breath, unless you fit into one of these special matchups.

❯*State Employment Commission.* This is a good place to touch base at the outset of your job search. The services offered will differ from state to state, so it is a good idea to make a call or visit to see what you actually can count on. Some of their counselors, for example, can be very helpful at the beginning of a transition period.

❯*Chamber of Commerce.* If you are moving to an unfamiliar town or area, here is a quick way to get a feel for available opportunities. It is not the Chamber's usual function to help job seekers, but it usually will have printed information on the large and medium-size companies in the area. Beyond that, it's up to you to find discreet ways to approach members of the Chamber, who have ties to all the key businesses in town. Call it the start of networking.

❯*Outplacement Services.* These are usually available on military bases at the family service centers, which have received large infusions of funds over the past five years or so. The quality of support offered by these centers will vary from base to base—but you would be remiss in not stopping by to see what the closest center has to offer. Because of recent funding decisions, there may be additional outplacement services available elsewhere on the base. Check them out. Remember that the motto of the job search is to leave no stone unturned.

❯*Military Associations.* The two largest are the Non-Commissioned Officers Association (NCOA), headquartered in San Antonio, Texas, with a branch in Alexandria, Virginia, and The Retired Officers Association (TROA), also located in Alexandria. In addition to lobbying for favorable legislation with respect to retired pay and benefits, these associations provide a number of services to their members, including outplacement assistance. Colonel Doug Carter, U.S. Air Force (Retired), the director of TROA's officer placement service (TOPS), delivers a superb two-and-one-half-hour lecture, "Marketing Yourself for a Second Career," at more than one hundred military installations every year for officers, noncommissioned officers, and their spouses. The lecture covers the realities of the civilian job market, rejection shock, résumé writing, networking, job-interview strategy, salary negotiation, and other related topics. Attend if you can.

Service-academy graduates can often find valuable networking assistance through their respective alumni associations, and the plethora of unit and ship's associations that exist today (just look at the reunion notes in any service-connected magazine) are another informal source of support. The Marine Corps alone has twenty-three such organizations in a loose confederation called the Marine Corps Council, as well as the Marine Executive Association, headquartered in McLean, Virginia, which helps Marines—officers and enlisted—build contacts and find employment on a nationwide scale.

❯*The Library.* The librarians got you started, when you went by to begin your preliminary exploration of career fields. As your search narrows, they can shift you to more-focused reference works, targeted on specific firms and organizations. Many libraries also carry a wide variety of trade journals and specialized publications, such as the *Wall Street Journal's National Business Employment Weekly,* which lists job opportunities throughout the country. If your local library does not have a specific reference, the chances are that the librarian can obtain it for you. Library systems are so interconnected today that your specific point of entry doesn't much matter.

For details, consult the Resource Directory in this book.

NETWORKING

Singly or in combination, these eight "normal" routes will lead you to the next step in your job search—establishing points of contact and lining up interviews. Such "networking" is the means through which 70 percent of the nation's job openings are filled.

You probably have used informal networking techniques in a number of ways. In buying a new or used car, for example, you undoubtedly checked around among friends who owned the type of vehicle you wanted, to see which makes and models performed best. You probably did some additional checking—directly and indirectly—to see which local dealerships offered the best sales-and-service packages, and which local lenders offered the best financing arrangement. Someone may have steered you to a particular salesman who could cut you a good deal. You even may have checked to see if a better deal could be made out of town. Some of the pieces of information and advice were undoubtedly more valuable than others; some probably were counterproductive; and some may have led nowhere. But by the time you finished, you most likely had constructed a solid network of timely, credible sources of advice to help you decide what type of vehicle to buy and where to buy it.

The principle is the same in job networking, except that you will be doing a lot of selling as well as buying. In addition to finding helpers, you want to create a *network of believers*—in you and in your quest. You can do this best by doing enough homework to narrow your career fields of interest to three or four before trying to set up a network of contacts. The most valuable members of this network, in terms of experience and range of contacts, are also most likely to be the busiest. One such individual, the executive director of a major national association, has been most generous with his valuable time in assisting military retirees in transition. A while back, he admitted to only one gripe: the job applicant who hasn't taken the time to figure out what he *might* want, much less what he really does want. After being shoehorned into the executive's tight schedule, the applicant walks in, takes a seat, and is asked the inevitable question:

"How can I help you? What type of career are you interested in?"

"Well, I can do a lot of things—something that pays well, I guess."

What a waste of time! And what an insult to the business executive. At the very beginning of the transition process, it is certainly okay to be vague about new careers. But after your self-evaluation workup, the chance to talk to career counselors and take career interest and preference tests, and other such preliminary steps, you should be in a position to sit before a high-powered executive and say:

"I have narrowed my search to these three fields, and would greatly appreciate any contacts you could provide in these areas."

More often than not, a response like that will bring results. And it will be time to tab a new section in your notebook:

CONTACTS

If you are looking into three different career fields, start three separate pages. Put the career field at the top and start logging in the contacts, with pertinent information:

CITY/MUNICIPAL MANAGEMENT

Cook, William G. (Bill) (wife—Barbara) Woodbridge, Virginia
> Referred by: Art Larson, American Soft Drink Association 3/94
> Has management contacts in Northern Virginia (Fairfax, Arlington, Prince William Counties)

❯ Phones: (W) (703) 555–5302
　　　　　(H) (703) 555–5446
❯ U.S. Marine Corps (Ret.)

Just keep adding to the list, as your contacts grow. Review your list(s) periodically, to think of new interconnections that already may be sitting in your notebook, waiting to be discovered.

After you have made your contact, be sure to write a brief thank-you note. A handwritten note on your personal stationery is fine, perhaps even better than an impeccably typed one:

> *Dear Bill,*
>
> *Many thanks for the introduction to Jay Hoffman, who provided a lot of good insights into recent changes in Northern Virginia county governments. Jay has given me some additional leads, which I am pursuing with vigor.*
>
> *You have provided a real boost to my new career search. I'll never forget your generosity with your time and thoughts.*
>
> *With best wishes,*

Notes like this have never failed to impress me. I find myself wanting to provide more assistance, any way I can. People like to be thanked for their efforts. It's that simple.

A SYSTEMATIC SEARCH

To get your "Contacts" file started, you need to do some systematic searching to recall the names of those who may be in a position to help you. Starting with your own address book and card file, expand your search to community and church address lists, social rosters from organizations to which you've belonged, alumni listings (especially ones updated for reunions), or any other stray collections of names you may have on hand. As you go through these lists, think about the last time you actually saw each person named and any conversations or interactions you had that might provide a link to the career fields that interest you. If you keep a datebook or calendar, work back through it to recall meetings, parties, vacations, and other nonroutine occasions when you met new people. Keep going back, for years if possible. You never can tell when a half-forgotten or long-forgotten name will jump out of your past.

After milking your written records for all they're worth, try a little creative scanning by category—relatives, military acquaintances, clubs and organizations, parents of your kids' friends, for example—to pick up any names that did not appear on your rosters.

From this point on, keep your notebook handy and add new prospective contacts as soon as possible after you run across their names. They may be people you read about, hear on the radio, or even see on television. They may come to you through a formal request for career information or through a chance remark.

Another thought: It's a good idea to maintain a backup file of three-by-five cards or even a home-computer file, alphabetized for easy reference, so the loss of your valuable notebook will not be a disaster. And even after a successful job search, you'll never know when you'll need such a comprehensive list of contacts again.

Because more than two out of three jobs are filled by networking, it follows that most of your time should be spent on this approach. Make sure you stay organized.

A FOOT IN THE DOOR: THE UNCOMMON WAYS

Job opportunities sometimes appear in out-of-the way places or under nonroutine circumstances:

›*Industry trade shows, conventions, and professional conferences.* Just about every major industry holds them. Some, like the computer shows, last a full week and move through a number of key cities. All of the top companies are represented, as well as some new kids on the block. Spending two or three days at a major trade show and talking to company representatives at their exhibit sites is a great way to find out what's going on in the industry, and what it would be like to work for individual firms—or their competition. For times and dates of shows in your region, look in trade magazines, contact one of the major companies, or check with your city's or state's convention and visitors bureau.

❯*Joining civic organizations.* Major organizations such as Lions, Kiwanis, Rotary, and Civitan can be found in every town of any size. Their luncheon and dinner meetings provide a good way to meet a cross section of the business and professional communities, and their philanthropic projects carry their members into still other aspects of community life, where they enjoy the respect of their neighbors. In this case, a commitment to community service can bring tangible as well as intangible rewards, through enhanced networking opportunities. Meeting times and places can be obtained from local newspapers, from sign boards at the entrance to town, or from the Chamber of Commerce.

❯*Working without pay.* This is a way to get your foot in the door, while finding out a lot about a possible line of work and how well you relate to it. An Army first sergeant from Fort Dix, New Jersey, who obtained his college diploma after seven years of off-duty study, got interested in newspaper work as a possible second career. During his final eighteen months of active duty, he got to know the editor of a small newspaper. He visited the paper's offices during off-duty hours and even spent a few days' leave time there, learning the ropes. He did odd jobs around the office, accompanied reporters on assignments, and asked hundreds of questions to learn more about the business. One day, he happened to be near the site of a major passenger-train derailment. Taking part in the rescue operations, he was moved by the courage and compassion of an elderly woman in caring for the injured at the scene. He wrote about it—not because he sought publication, but because he just had to put the story into writing. Later, he showed it to his editor, who promptly published it. The story drew praise from the readers, and the first sergeant was hooked. Brimming with confidence, he began to write other pieces for publication. After retiring from the Army, he went back home to the Boston area and hooked up with a medium-size newspaper, where he is now the city editor. And it all started when he worked for nothing—or did he?

❯*Recognizing corporate problems.* A major stationed at Fort Campbell, Kentucky, had decided that he would retire in the Minneapolis-St. Paul area. His wife got him a subscription to a Twin Cities newspaper, so he could follow his beloved Vikings football team and get a feel for the job market. Going through the paper, he read that a county in the suburbs had just hired a new superintendent of schools, who faced a number of problems—one of which was upgrading the county's decrepit school bus system. The major wrote the new superintendent, outlining a series of similar problems he had solved in the Army and stating how he would approach the school bus procurement and maintenance situation, together with the hiring and training of new drivers. He presented himself as a uniquely qualified problem solver, and flew to Minnesota at his own expense to confer with the superintendent and members of the school board, creating a highly favorable impression. He remained in contact with them for the remaining five months before his retirement. With a month to go, he was offered a position.

In another more altruistic example, a Navy chief petty officer stationed at New London, Connecticut, read an article in the local paper about a nearby marina that had been besieged with problems ever since the death of its owner. The chief offered his help to the widow, and after putting in long off-duty hours and weekends, he managed to get the marina back into a profitable condition. After he retired from the Navy a year or so later, the widow offered him part ownership.

❯*Making a speech.* A Marine gunnery sergeant from Mississippi, serving with a Marine Corps Reserve unit in New England, was heavily involved with the unit's annual Toys-for-Tots Christmas drive for underprivileged children. He would start soliciting each September for toy donations from schools, corporations, and civic organizations. On one occasion, he was invited to speak at a Chamber of Commerce luncheon to roughly one hundred business and community leaders about the program, but declined, offering the services of his commanding officer instead. On the morning of the luncheon, his CO had to accompany his wife on an unscheduled trip to the hospital, so the gunny had to pinch-hit. He knew the Toys-for-Tots program from top to bottom, but this first trip to the microphone had him uneasy. After announcing that his talk would be given in a foreign accent, he confided to his audience that there were two situations he prayed he'd never get into. "One is facing a company of civilians, and the other is facing them alone in enemy territory," he said. The warm laughter broke the ice and the gunny was on his way. Over the next two years, he gave more than twenty speeches about Toys-for-Tots, as contributions tripled. And when he retired, he received four offers of employment from local firms.

The military profession is held in high regard across the nation, and military speakers are generally well received, especially in areas where there is no major military presence. Civic organizations trying to line up interesting programs for their luncheon and dinner meetings are interested in military speakers on both military and nonmilitary (for example, a community approach to the war on drugs) topics. If you are enthusiastic and knowledgeable, and pack a good sense of humor you will do well with most local audiences. If you want more polish, you can join a Toastmasters club or take a Dale Carnegie public-speaking course. And yes—by presenting yourself to the business and professional community as articulate and well informed, you can generate interviews and job offers for yourself.

›*Volunteering.* A Coast Guard wife showed me a notebook she and her husband start and maintain at each duty station. The book opens with a page each for their individual interests: she likes making pottery, gardening, working on school committees, doing Red Cross work, and making extra money as a temporary employee with her typing skill; he likes computers, skeet shooting, vintage cars, Civil War history, and politics. These pastimes are followed by a page of their joint interests—square dancing, bowling, gourmet cooking, and studying the Bible. At each new duty station, they search out organizations and activities that tie in with their interests.

Their notebook soon begins to build up, with a separate section for each activity containing names, addresses, phone numbers, children's names, and other information about their new contacts. Serving on boards and supporting political candidates have seemed to produce the best business contacts for the couple. In addition, the wife's part-time work for the temporary employment agency gets her an inside look at a number of local firms. This couple is creating a reservoir of good will through their volunteer work, while getting a leg up on retirement opportunities in fields they enjoy. Somehow, I have a feeling that they will land on their feet in CivLand, when their Coast Guard days are over.

❯*Advertising yourself.* The following ad ran twice a week for six weeks:

> EMPLOYMENT WANTED
>
> Energetic, responsible, intelligent individual with distinguished background is relocating to Columbia area.
> Looking for career that will allow use of exceptional interpersonal and organizational skills.
> Proven track record:
> ❯ Operating effectively under stressful conditions—
> ❯ As a team player
> ❯ As a communicator.
> Possesses strong basic technical skills; learns quickly
> Edward D. Sawyer
> 91 Selden Avenue, Bremerton, Washington
> (206) 555–2002

Ed chose not to mention his military background in the ad. Although this type of advertisement is generally not effective (because employers seldom read employment-wanted ads), Ed's ad produced five inquiries during its six-week run because of the way he chose to showcase it. His three-by-three ad ran in the business section, rather than the classified section. Employment-wanted ads tend to get lost in the classified section of most papers, and could be costly if run as display.

❯*Riding your hobby horse.* Combining business with pleasure is, of course, the ultimate in any career choice. One part-time artist in San Diego realized with some frustration that the art world was not beating down his door, as his military career drew to an end. But after some digging he discovered to his surprise and joy that related career opportunities in the field existed in abundance: framing, selling art supplies, and working for art-auction companies, for example. After careful examination of the alternatives, he settled in with a major art-auction company in New York.

❯*Attention to detail.* A helicopter crew chief compiled a list of component parts he worked with in his aircraft—e.g., winches, slings, seats, rotor blades—and wrote to their manufacturers, making upbeat comments on the good features of the equipment and offering constructive criticism wherever things could be improved. He followed up this correspondence by visiting some of the smaller (50 to 150 employees) companies. Well-dressed, he told the receptionists that he had information to share with the company presidents about their equipment's performance during search-and-rescue operations. This invariably was well received by the companies, and enabled him to network into other interviews—one of which landed him a job.

❯*Going to the source.* Another effective networking technique is to read carefully articles about your chosen field in periodicals, especially trade publications—then contact the authors to ask about their sources—which often prove to be key contacts in industry.

❯*A word of caution.* You never know when or where you will meet someone who can help network you into an interview with the employer of your dreams. So be ready at all times with your own thirty- to sixty-second spot commercial—a quick rundown of your skills, talents, and capabilities—for anyone who might forward your name to the right firm. *Never forget,* however, that the purpose of an informational networking interview is not to land a job with that interviewer but to present your credentials and ask for contacts that will lead to a job offer. Asking a networking contact for a job is the kiss of death—you will get neither a new job nor new contacts.

> *Creative marketing.* Some career seekers have taken things into their own hands, with great success. In two separate instances, an Air Force captain (female) from the Southeast and a Navy petty officer (male) from the Northwest each took thirty days' leave and traveled through several states in their regions. They dropped in, unannounced, on dozens of companies. At the end of their travels, each had received multiple job offers.

They had done their homework, using basic library reference tools plus the *Directory of Manufacturers,* which—in a separate volume for each state—lists companies both by industry and by location, describing them in terms of size, products, and salary ranges, among other things. After indentifying their target companies, they planned their itineraries. They chose to steer clear of major corporations in large cities, whose personnel or human-resources departments would not be expected to smile kindly upon drop-in job seekers.

Dressed in business attire (*not* their uniforms, no matter how sharp or well decorated) and armed with their crisp, clear résumés and their own thirty-second commercials, they walked up to company receptionists with big smiles and a pitch something like this:

"Hi! I'm Mary Jones and I'm winding up a career in the Air Force. I am checking out career opportunities in your industry, and would really like to talk with someone in your personnel department while I'm here in town."

Such an approach should contain the following key points:

> You are a member of the armed forces. In the wake of Desert Storm and the humanitarian operations in Bangladesh and Somalia, the military services enjoy a reservoir of good will throughout the country. The chances are at least one in five that the receptionist will have a good friend or relative in one of the services, possibly yours.

> You have traveled some distance to get there. In other words, you have gone out of your way to visit that particular company.

❯ You make an impression of sharpness—well dressed, with an energetic, outgoing personality.
❯ You know something about the company (a product of your careful research).

If you choose your targets carefully, do your homework, and show genuine interest in your first encounter with each company, the drop-in technique can provide a better-than-even chance of getting an interview. Once there, if you hear that the company "isn't hiring right now," don't lose the networking opportunity that may still exist. Ask about who may be hiring, and gather the names of additional contacts. And don't give up on a company before you have checked it out thoroughly. You might know in advance that a firm is downsizing and laying off engineers, accountants, and front-office staff—but you may *not* know that they are looking for new talent in their marketing or procurement ranks.

Another thing you may have to discover on scene is that your target company (usually one of the smaller, leaner ones) may be looking for multipurpose utility fielders who can cover several bases: running the purchasing department, helping with marketing and advertising, and even making sales calls, if needed. Your varied military background may be just what *they* need; just be sure the matchup meets *your* needs.

Is there any lower limit to the size of companies you should check out? Well, yes. A company of twenty-five or more employees is probably out of its most-vulnerable infancy stage and may possibly be growing—or at least it's getting serious.

NONTRADITIONAL ... OR OFF-THE-WALL?

We all can recall some bigger-than-life characters from our service days—and some have carried their flamboyant ways into the job-search effort. Take this true example of a mustang captain, retiring from the Air Force after twenty years:

To be sure that he covered all the bases on his planned return home to Oklahoma, he hired a public-relations firm. The firm's first act was to sign him up with the American Legion, which in turn invited him to be the grand marshal of his home town's Memorial Day parade. This, of course, meant a feature story above the fold on the front page of the local paper, and coverage on the six o'clock television news. Then came a few radio and television talk-show appearances, some news releases, speaking engagements with the Lions and Rotary clubs and the Chamber of Commerce, and a sports-page picture and feature story of our hero throwing out the first pitch of the Little League season. As he basked in the limelight, he was networking with his newfound friends in the community and before long some glowing third-party letters of endorsement were finding their way to presidents and CEOs of some of the area's leading companies. Interviews and job offers followed.

Total cost of this public-relations blitz: three thousand one hundred dollars.

Is this approach recommended for everyone? Certainly not. But if the urge hits you to do something a little bit crazy at some point during your job-search campaign, don't discard the idea out of hand. Think it through. What do you stand to lose? And what do you stand to gain?

WHAT IS THE ``RIGHT`` APPROACH?

Whatever works for you.

Many factors will bear on the approach you take—the state of the job market locally, the state of the economy in general, and your own timetable (carefully developed, or an eleventh-hour matter), among other things.

But if you have pinpointed one career (or several) that you want to explore, and if you have focused your networking efforts in that direction, then sooner or later things will begin to fall into place:

> Your eyes will go automatically toward and focus clearly on advertisements in your field of interest;

> You will target the right companies in the right geographical area;
> You will get through the front doors of some of those companies, either through a network contact or a résumé and cover letter;
> You will be alert to corporate changes or problems that could launch you into a creative action plan;
> And, in time, you will find your matchup.

Don't be bashful. If you see a job out there you really want— *go for it!* Become a virtual hound dog, to track down the right contacts. Be willing to take some risks, if necessary, in your approach. You might have the same good fortune as the retired Army nurse who was making casual conversation with the man in the seat next to hers, on a flight from San Francisco to Denver, and mentioned that she would like to get into the medical sales field. The man, who worked for a major pharmaceutical company, gave her his card and told her to call him at work. She did, went on to be interviewed by the regional sales manager, and slid easily into her own Phase II.

Don't prejudge people. We all are guilty of this at times. An Air Force wife, at a mixed military-civilian cocktail party at Georgia's Dobbins Air Force Base, fell into conversation with a beefy "Bubba" type who loved to talk about his favorite college football team, but still managed to ask her what she and her husband planned to do upon retirement. They both wanted to teach—she in high school, he in college. Later in the evening the Bubba, who happened to be the president of a major Southern university, left his card with her, and eventually proved instrumental in getting both of them launched in their teaching careers.

HANG IN THERE

I have seen and heard of many cases where persistence, enthusiasm, and a sense of humor have carried the day. As an employer and recruiter, I always have favored these qualities.

Just remember the man from Barnum & Bailey.

7
....

PREPARING FOR
THE INTERVIEW

C harisma is the personal magnetic quality that endears you to
others and causes them to trust you, believe in you, and follow
you. The armed forces have long acknowledged "born" leaders,
who seem to project charisma effortlessly. Nevertheless, the services also have managed, over the years, to develop effective
"made" leaders at all echelons, through teaching, study, and much
individual effort.

As a job seeker, you must project charisma—or confidence, at
least—in any interview with a potential employer. So what else is
new? As a military leader, you have been called upon to do that
from the beginning. Most of us can recall the outstanding leaders
we have seen and tried to emulate. Some were flamboyant; others
were quiet, yet forceful. They stayed within their personalities, pro-
jecting sincerity. And the common denominator they shared was
that they knew themselves and they knew their business. Their resulting self-assurance was picked up and adopted by the men and
women they led, so that in time the entire unit would bear the stamp
of its commander's personality, trying to match the leader's desire
to excel.

Up to this point, we have worked together to sharpen your self-
knowledge, and with it your self-assurance, as we reviewed your
strengths, weaknesses, goals, and even dreams. You should feel as
though you are on firm ground now, with respect to what you want

to do for the rest of your life and the skills and talents you are bringing to this career search. Now that you are just about ready to walk through the interviewer's door with a smile that radiates poise, confidence, and sincerity, it's time for a quick look at your image and style.

Whenever I interview, the candidates—men and women—who walk through that doorway first appear to me like Bo Derek walking out of the surf at Acapulco. Every one of them is a perfect "ten." The slate is clean. In fact, the slate is even better than clean, because either a strong résumé or someone's personal recommendation has caused this interview to take place, and I always hope that the person I am about to interview will turn out to be the right one for the job. Interviewing is hard work. I try to examine in depth the histories of all candidates, to ensure that they are wired together correctly and are bringing the right combination of experience, talent, and skills to the job. Whenever I uncover a weak area, I will probe around until I can tell whether there is a true cause for concern. All the while, deep inside, I am rooting for the candidates in front of me—especially if they have military backgrounds. Most of the interviewers you will face feel the same way I do—even those without military service of their own. They want to be impressed.

Despite all these factors in your favor, there are any number of potential flaws in your appearance, bearing, or style that can drop you out of your perfect "ten" rating and torpedo your interview, no matter how well everything else goes. These image busters, which seldom fail to turn off interviewers everywhere, fall into seven general areas: poor grooming, annoying habits, undignified bearing, irritating or indistinct voice patterns, inappropriate body language, lack of basic manners, and incorrect attire. Some of my observations may seem only too obvious, but they weren't obvious to *someone* going into an interview, or else they would not have become notorious in my business as examples of what not to do. Once you're aware of them, you can make any needed corrections after a quick inspection before a mirror. To *become* aware of them, however, you might want to get help from your spouse or an acquaintance with a video camera. Friends may want to spare your feelings. The camera doesn't care about your feelings. It tells you only what it sees.

The late Gilda Radner had a comic persona called Roseann Rosannadanna, who could not get close to the rich and famous without becoming loudly aware of the small—usually disgusting—physical flaws of the celebrities. The act worked because it sounded a note of recognition in the audience. It rang deliciously true, both in its human tendency to take delight in finding warts on the beautiful people and to be so fascinated by imperfection that all other thoughts—no matter how much more elevated—were driven out. Well, here's a real-life example: A personnel director was interviewing a sharp, well-dressed man and things were going well until he turned his head—and a blob of ear wax landed on her desk! "I can't remember a thing he said after that," she told me. "I kept looking at that little piece of wax on my desk, to see if it was going to move."

If this could never happen to you—great! You will have no trouble with this chapter, as you accompany me through the minefield of potential appearance destroyers. Consider my observations as a cautionary tale. If you feel particularly vulnerable in one or more areas, however, a great number of image-enhancing books are out there to take you into greater depth. For a starter list, consult our Resource Directory in the back of this book.

GROOMING FOR CIVLAND

Let's take it from the top, and talk about hair (for those of you who still have enough left). Unless your position allows or requires you to wear your military uniform to work—legally—forget about the high-and-tight, white-sidewall look or, for women, hair pulled back severely in a bow. The look of the shaggy sixties and seventies also is generally out, unless you are seeking specialized employment in the entertainment world. The upshot is that there is an up-to-date, appropriate hair style for you out there somewhere that probably will be acceptable at your future workplace. Find out how the executives in your prospective firm are groomed. If you cannot, safe-side things and go conservative: hair about two or three inches long on top and tapered at the sides for men, and medium-length or short hair parted on the side for women. Adopting such a look also might help wean some of you away from once-a-week haircuts at the post exchange.

Next, check your eyebrows. If they look like hedgerows, use the scissors or tweezers on them—or get your barber or hair stylist to do it. I remember asking a man who had grown one giant eyebrow, bushy enough to hang his hat on, why he didn't trim it. "Oh, that gets people's attention," he said. "They never forget who I am." He was right. I never have forgotten him. The problem is that I can't remember anything else about him.

And men, while you're at it, get your barber to go after any tufts of hair that may be sprouting from your ears like clumps of weeds in a railroad yard or any attention grabbers that may be dangling from your nose. Women should pluck any hairs that sprout from moles on the chin or face. And don't forget that little bouncing ball of wax. If wax buildup is a real problem, ear-flushing kits are available at your nearest drugstore.

A warm, engaging smile is hard to present if you are in obvious need of dental work. While you are still on active duty, you have your last opportunity to become best of friends with your dentist, without taking out a second mortgage on your home.

Finally, check your hands. Clean, trimmed fingernails are a must, of course—but do you have creeping cuticles that push halfway up the nails? Soak them in warm water, push them back, and trim them. Or spring for a manicure and learn how a pro does it. Well-manicured nails are an especially nice finishing touch for women, but make sure the color of any nail polish is not too strong—like red. During an interview, you should be able to use your hands with all the confidence of a fighter pilot.

These uncomfortably personal matters are included in this book because very few of even your best friends are likely to mention them in your presence. And the sad fact is that I've seen hundreds of candidates who needed to be aware of them—and weren't. You are putting in a lot of work to be able to see your way clear to your employment objectives, all the way across the crowded room. As you begin to make your move, make certain that you don't trip over a piece of furniture right off the bat.

BEARING AND DEMEANOR

Please take this example to heart: A ranking executive from a leading pharmaceutical company once came to my office to interview three candidates for an open sales territory he wanted to fill. I had met two of the candidates prior to the interview, and was convinced that they were competitive. The third, however, was so well qualified on paper that I considered him the shoo-in for the job. I just told him over the telephone where and when to show up for the employer's interview.

But when he walked into the office, my heart sank. Maybe he was just trying to be cool, but his stooped posture and weary shuffle made him look as though he'd just completed a midsummer twenty-five-mile hike with full field pack.

As the employer said later, "He lost the job when he walked in the door. He was well qualified, and well informed about our company and its products, but the weary way he entered the room told me that he either was a burnout case, or on the verge of becoming one." The candidate was only thirty-eight years old.

A regimental commander once said, "One thing I cannot stand is a tired lieutenant." The captains of industry feel the same way.

WATCH YOUR WORDS

"Mastin—you talk funny!" was a comment from my drill instructor that really got my attention during my first week at boot camp.

Somehow, my New York accent and idioms were not playing well in the Deep South.

A regional accent, in itself, may well be beyond your control. But you can do something about the pitch, intonation, and speech patterns of your voice—not to put on a phony act, but to sound *your* best, the way *you* want to be perceived. Your "voice," which includes your appearance and mannerisms as well as your speech, is not something you put on for the occasion. It comes from the inside out, sounding as clear, energetic, calm, interested, and lively as you truly are about getting started in your new career.

Make an audio-tape cassette, preferably one that records you in unrehearsed conversation. Will you like what you hear? Unless you are a professional radio announcer, you probably won't. You will hear halting speech patterns, sentence fragments, an annoying laugh, a grating high-pitched voice, or perhaps an overuse of clichés.

On the other hand, your interview voice may not antagonize anyone, but it may induce sleep instead. As one retiring colonel commented, after hearing his practice-interview tape: "Good grief—that's the most unexciting person I have ever heard." His monotone and barely audible voice failed to project the hard-charging image he wanted to create.

While you are working on the voice, check out the words. Proper terminology and knowledge of military minutiae may be hallmarks of the professional soldier, but they don't count for much outside the gate. In fact, they may serve only to convince interviewers that you are still hanging on to your old life—not ready to step into Phase II. So try your best to change decks into floors, latrines and heads into bathrooms, and campaign objectives into goals, projects, or sales targets.

It's also time to check the scatological content of your conversation. If you swear like a trooper—and if watching R-rated movies and blue stand-up comedy on late-night cable television has convinced you that the whole world talks dirty—think again. If your conversational language descends occasionally to the cesspool

level, start working on it *now*. You may think that you'll be able
to switch frequencies cleanly when it's time to walk into the interview room, but as you focus on the substance of the questions and
answers, the worst words have a way of slipping into your conversation at the worst possible time. I have seen it happen. Don't
let it happen to you.

Finally, remember that the expression on your face tells the interviewer how to interpret your words. When an experienced counselor told me this in the mid-1970s, I rejected the notion. But during
the intervening years, as both a recruiter and an outplacement specialist, I have become a believer. Faces do reveal insecurity, sup-
pressed anger, even outright fear—no matter what is being said in
words. So what are you supposed to do—have a face lift? No . . .
faces also can reveal warmth and inner strength. Start changing
your face from within, by clarifying in your own mind who you
are and whom you want to become.

ANNOYING MANNERISMS

No matter how hard an interviewer tries, it is difficult to stay focused on the conversation if annoying habits or mannerisms inter-
vene. Maybe someone has told you about your distracting twitches
and quirks—in a kidding way, of course. Or perhaps no one has
ever told you, out of concern for your bruised feelings or possibly
fear of your anger. All I can say is that after years of interviewing,
I can tell you about the ear pickers, and the head scratchers, and
the nail biters, and the watch watchers. But I can't tell you much
about them, because I can't remember anything else.

BODY LANGUAGE

If you took off your insignia of rank, could you still inspire your
troops to forge ahead with you for the greater good of your outfit?
Would they be captured by the strength of your personality and
ideals?

Everyone likes to be associated with a winner—someone who radiates success and strength, and who has it all together. The core ingredient of charisma is enthusiasm—the call to action that binds people to their ideals. Enthusiasm is contagious, and brings people around to your way of thinking. It makes things happen.

Interviewers can see enthusiasm in your eyes, and they will not fail to pick it up in your body language. So they are certain to detect a lack of enthusiasm in a slouch, a tired head in your hand, a lazy gesture, or even a disapproving look when a new idea is broached—accompanied by crossed arms across the chest, the classic signal of skepticism.

Don't be afraid to err on the side of enthusiasm. You'll be able to feel it in your bones, and you will see its charismatic impact in your interviewers' eyes.

MIND YOUR MANNERS

After a rough patch over the past few decades, the business world has rediscovered the importance of good manners in bringing domestic and overseas customers to their firms. More than 500 companies across the nation now provide courses in executive etiquette. In addition, more than 250 image-consulting firms have sprung up across the country. The picture is clear: to be competitive, you need to have your act together in many ways—how you look, what you wear, what you say, and how you say it.

It is generally accepted that manners are acquired habits, but that they should be exercised as though they were inherent attributes—a product of the genes, almost. Experts agree that manners should be sincere and inclusive—predicated on kindness and consideration for others—rather than ''who's smarter?'' drills designed to exclude and humiliate those who may have less schooling in manners.

If you take to heart the philosophy of kindness and consideration as the underpinning of good manners, you won't go far wrong in most social situations. The question of manners boils down to a series of small decisions you must make as you move through the day. Here are a few examples of situations where newer forms of corporate etiquette are replacing more traditional ones:

❯*Using first names.* To anyone accustomed to a relatively strict hierarchy of rank (although the strictness tends to vary among units and even among military services), it must seem as though everyone in CivLand is on a first-name basis. Such appearances can be deceiving, for the hierarchy still exists and just about everyone knows his or her place in it, without external cues such as insignia of rank. Quite often, junior and senior executives will first-name each other if they have worked together for a while or if the senior has given permission—and they both feel comfortable with the arrangement. When in doubt, it's better to err on the side of formality, until you've been asked to "call me Joe."

❯*Shaking hands.* A firm, full handshake—not just the tips of the fingers—upon meeting and departing is the norm for both genders. No bonecrushers, please—ever!

❯*Taking seats.* In an unfamiliar situation, wait to be told where to sit. It is always appropriate to stand when greeting a visitor of either gender (you are going to shake hands, aren't you?) and stand again when the visitor or senior corporate leadership leave the room. When in doubt, follow the lead of the one in charge.

❯*Grabbing the check.* It is perfectly appropriate for either gender—the inviter pays. In an ambiguous situation, when you wish to establish early on that you will pick up the check, just tell the waiter, "My guests and I are ready to order."

❯*Leaving the elevator.* Let common sense prevail. If the elevator is crowded, men need not shuffle around to let women out first. The person closest to the door should lead the way.

❯*Making conversation.* To break the ice with strangers, I have always felt most comfortable trying to find out something interesting about the other person or group. Once you discover areas of mutual interest, the conversation flows naturally. If you have a natural sense of humor, let it come through. Remember, though, that few of us are accomplished stand-up comedians. If you can't deliver a punch line, stay away from canned jokes. And, especially in today's supercharged climate, stay completely away from off-color, ethnic, or sexist jokes—unless you'd enjoy serving as a horrible example.

❯*Saying good-bye.* Empty etiquette is never appropriate, because it's an airheaded substitute for the real thing. The next time you tell someone to "Have a nice day," I hope he or she responds, "Sorry, but I have other plans"—to get you thinking again. If you can't speak with sincerity, it might be better to say nothing at all.

Good manners will not vault you into the highest realms of business life automatically, but I have seen and heard of hiring and promotion situations in which a candidate's demeanor has been the tiebreaker—where experience, education, and all other factors have been a wash. I also have seen and heard of situations where inadvertent displays of bad manners have been game enders, and I don't want that to happen to any of you.

LOOKING SHARP

For years, the conventional wisdom has been that a military retiree, with or without longer hair, is a real standout—in the worst sense of the word—in civilian clothes. Let's work together to put an end to that myth.

Let's face it: When we attempt to color coordinate clothing, some of us have the visual equivalent of a tin ear. If you have a knack for wearing clashing combinations that people can hear for blocks around, there is only one thing to do—seek out an expert. Your clothing guru might be your spouse, who can help you shop for the right clothing, then lay it out in appropriate combinations once you get it home. You might get help from someone in your present workplace who is generally recognized as a sharp dresser. You might strike up a friendship with a knowledgeable salesperson at a reputable clothing store or with an image consultant. In other words, you need to find someone who can teach you the fine points of determining quality in clothing, as well as help you coordinate colors, patterns, and textures that are right for you. With a combination of expert help and your own powers of observation—analyzing window displays and taking a discerning look at what people are wearing in the business you are targeting and in the street, for example, you can get on top of this problem quickly.

Now that we know the goal is attainable, let's set about building a basic wardrobe. What you get depends upon where you are going. If you are headed for a *Fortune* 500 board room in New York City, you are looking at some top-of-the-line, custom-tailored suits, just for openers. On the other hand, you may be angling for a county agent's job in the Texas Panhandle. Then you can save all that "sincere suit" expense and put the money into a down payment on the pickup truck of your dreams.

Most of us, of course, fall somewhere in between the Big Apple and Donley County. And in making the in-between choices, the thing to remember is that the wardrobe must match the job. Most professions have a "look" of their own—as do different parts of the country. Before you invest a couple months' pay in a new wardrobe, do your best to find out which new look will be the right one for you in your new workplace. You might keep yourself from buying some things that you will never take out of the closet after one wearing.

Once you have determined your requirements, it's time to take inventory—emptying out your closets for a real "junk on the bunk" inspection. This is the time to clean house. What about that polyester suit you have been lugging around for the past twenty years? Or those shiny white plastic loafers that you wore with your bell-bottoms? Those skin-tight custom silk shirts from Hong Kong have to go, too.

If you have the time and inclination, you can raise your level of expertise before you ever step into a clothing store to build your wardrobe. You can read fashion magazines and dressing-for-success books and articles; you can attend clothing seminars and fashion shows; you even can become a window-shopping expert. But your best bet for making wise purchases is still finding a quality retail store that carries a wide selection of traditionally styled, well-tailored clothing. You will be looking for fine natural fabrics: quality wools, wool blends, cottons, and silks. Don't be afraid to ask questions. If the sales force at your chosen store cannot or will not give you the answers you seek, find another store. You won't regret it, over the long run.

An associate of mine from Chicago managed to develop a system that overcame his total dread of shopping for clothes. Once a year, he would build into his schedule a morning at his favorite clothing store in New York, as a side excursion during one of his business trips. His favorite salesman at that store always knew when he was coming, was thoroughly familiar with his preferences in style, and had a fairly good fix on his annual needs. He would always be ready at the appointed hour with a selection of suits, shirts, ties, and even socks. As the businessman sorted through the selection, he and the salesman had coffee and a snack, and caught up on the preceding year's events. In two hours or so, this customer would walk out smiling, outfitted for another year.

There's another thing to consider before you step into the store. I have already alluded to the need to coordinate colors among the various pieces of your wardrobe; there also must be awareness of your distinctive combination of skin, eye, and hair coloring.

Author Carole Jackson has pointed out that nature's four distinct seasons have their own palettes of colors. Every individual has natural coloring—in hair, skin, and eyes—that harmonizes with one of these seasons. Discovering the right palette can do wonders for anyone's appearance and self-confidence. This notion has caught on like wildfire. Women have been lining up ever since to ''get their colors done.'' One resourceful Marine wife even marched her six nieces over to her brother-in-law's hardware store, and did their colors by lining them up against the charts of paint samples on display there.

The natural tendency is to think that this concept applies only to women—who, after all, have more leeway in adjusting eye, hair, and skin tones. But it works for men, as well. I discovered that my own skin tone tends to be pale, so wearing white shirts just washes me out. I look much better in blue or off-white shirts. So with the help of a book—or a friend, or a professional—check out your coloring, and take some of the guesswork out of assembling your wardrobe.

GO FOR QUALITY

Now, it's time to start building the wardrobe. For the sake of argument, let's assume that your inspection has weeded out all the antiques and you are essentially starting from accessories. But for most of us in less-opulent business surroundings, the next stop after the basic "sincere" suit is the classic navy-blue blazer, with gray trousers in a couple of shades. You should be able to wear this outfit with any combination of shirts, ties, and socks you have assembled for your basic suit. But don't wear it to the interview, unless you are certain that the hiring company has such an informal dress code that wearing a suit would ruin your chances.

ADDITIONAL TIPS

Here are a few more random hints (remember, books have been written about all of this, and you can begin with our Resource Directory if you wish to pursue matters further):

❯A pinstripe suit helps short men look taller. The vertical line formed by the classic three-button jacket, together with pockets that point inward and upward, will enhance that illusion.

❯A two-button suit will help create a slender appearance.

❯Vests are out.

❯Even though cuffs are coming back, shorter men should avoid them, as well as wide trousers.

❯Dark suits make heavy men look thinner.

❯Very thin men should play down the vertical lines (including pinstripes) and look for ways to enhance the horizontal dimension. One way is by using thicker and nubbier fabrics. Another is to wear patterns in layers (e.g., a patterned shirt under a plaid suit).

❯ White shirts are making a comeback in more conservative business settings. A white shirt can pull an entire look together, complimenting brighter and bolder ties especially well. In less-formal settings, men have a wider selection in shirt colors. Dark shirts are popular in the arts and retail fields, and pastel shirts are appropriate almost anywhere.

❯ Whatever the shirt's color, the button-down collar is relatively informal, and is not recommended for the interview. Button downs tend to wrinkle when worn with a tie. The best look comes from nonbutton-down collars that lie flat against the shirt.

❯ The best look you can wear comes from a 100-percent-cotton shirt, professionally laundered with just a little starch.

❯ Don't wear white polyester shirts. They tend to go gray after several washings and they look cheap.

❯ Double-check your neck size and sleeve length. Gravity sets in over time. You need one quarter inch to one half inch of cuff showing beneath the jacket sleeve.

❯ Don't even think about scrimping when you go out to purchase a tie. Quality really counts here, because the right tie sets off your entire appearance. If at all possible, select your ties with the suit-and-shirt combination you'll be wearing close at hand. You can't go wrong on shades then.

❯ Use an elegant overhand or four-in-hand knot (the Windsor knot went out a generation ago). If you are accustomed to putting a dimple below the knot in your military ties, keep it up; it looks sharp in CivLand, too. At the right length, your tie should come down to your belt buckle.

❯ As you develop different looks with your shirt and tie combinations, be sure to include at least one "power" tie, with a reddish background—for that look of authority when you sit down to negotiate your salary. Paisley is good for achieving this look.

❯ A relatively plain loafer is a more up-to-date shoe choice than the traditional wing tip, unless you are trying to project a super-conservative image. You are out of the violent spit-shine business, but the shoes should be well polished, especially in the heel area that tends to scuff first. And what about your super-shiny Corfam uniform shoes? Save 'em for the Veterans Day parade. Finally, no holes in the soles, please. The famous Adlai Stevenson mid-1950s look went out with . . . Adlai Stevenson.

❯ Your socks should reach to midcalf or higher, and be at least as dark as your trouser legs in a solid color (or a very subtle pattern). Any leg showing, even a tanned one, is a turnoff.

❯ When it comes to jewelry, keep it simple. I'll never forget the proud veteran who showed up for an interview in Southern California wearing three personal-decoration lapel pins, an American flag pin, a jump-wings tie bar, and a king-size service ring on each hand. I wish someone had told him to keep it functional—wedding ring, school ring, maybe a tie tack if it is smart and small. Avoid jewelry that advertises your pet cause(s). You are there to sell yourself, not your cause, to the interviewer.

❯ Carry a good pen and/or pencil in your inside coat pocket, not in your shirt pocket.

❯ If you wear glasses, don't wear any that will be dark enough to shade your eyes from the interviewer, or on any other occasion where direct eye contact is essential. And make sure they are clean, please.

LOOKING SHARP—HERS

Women can build a basic business wardrobe, too. According to Robyn Winters, a nationally recognized image consultant, the basic wardrobe begins with a solid neutral-color suit. As with men, navy blue is safe—no matter what the "season" of the wearer. Also, please:

❯ Choose a classic style (simple, unornamented) in a quality fabric such as wool or silk.

❯ Team this with a coordinating-color blouse in a fabric that blends with the suit (e.g., cotton or silk with a wool suit; silk or rayon with a silk suit). The blouse should be tailored—not too casual, not too dressy—and should feel comfortable.

❯ If appropriate for the interview and the company, you may wear a jacket or blazer coordinated with a skirt and blouse, in lieu of a suit.

❯ Select shoes that are leather or patent leather in a color that complements your suit, in a medium-heel pump. Avoid open-toed or sling-back heels; they may give the wrong impression. Make sure that the heel lifts are not worn to bare metal that will click when you walk across uncarpeted areas.

❯ Don't wear pantyhose that are darker than your shoes; i.e., don't wear beige, bone, or white shoes with dark stockings—they just don't blend well.

❯ Accessories—a ring, bracelet, and/or watch—add a nice touch, but don't overdo them. Dangling, jangling bracelets, for example, can focus the interviewer's attention on the wrong thing.

❯ Fragrance should be used *in moderation*. A strong scent is a turnoff. [Men—that goes for your cologne or aftershave, too!]

❯ A final thought—nothing shows up more vividly than dandruff on the shoulders of a navy-blue suit. Plenty of products are available over the counter to take care of that problem—for men, too.

A FINAL REMINDER

You have the power to control and improve virtually everything I have talked about in this chapter. I have described a minefield of potential disasters, but if you locate and neutralize the mines in advance, you can cross that field with confidence, instead of faking your way through, hoping for a miracle.

The chances are that the interviewer you face will never have worn a military uniform. Remember, we have had an all-volunteer force for more than twenty years. But almost all interviewers will have a high regard for military service and will have high expectations of you. Most likely, they will start you at the same "ten" level I would assign if I were doing the interview.

So do your homework and find out who you are . . . pay attention to the details . . . walk into that interview room with the confidence born of self-knowledge . . . and sail through the interview, keeping your "ten" intact—all the way!

8

THE INTERVIEW

This is it! It's your time to step into the batter's box.

The baseball analogy fits. Once in the box, you must perform within its confines and by the rules of the game. The best way to get out of the box is to make a hit—preferably a home run, but a triple or double or even a scratch single will keep you in the game. It's a big mistake, however, to enter the interview room looking for a base on balls. You have to take a healthy cut at the ball, to show the interviewer how good you are and why you belong on his team.

There's another difference. The interviewer is not the star pitcher from the rival ball club across town, determined to strike you out. He is more like a coach from the team you are trying to join. He would like nothing better than to see you hit a home run—but he is not going to feed you an easy series of soft pitches to knock over the fence. His job is to test your mettle, and he will generally do it in a straightforward way, but the rules allow him to throw you a curve ball every now and then, to see how you react.

Despite these minor differences, there is a major parallel with the game of baseball: When you step into the batter's box, you are alone. The game, in all its dimensions, has narrowed momentarily into a one-on-one contest between you and the pitcher. You bring to this moment all the basic talent, skills, coaching, determination, and other preparation and support you have been able to acquire.

But no one else can swing that bat for you. Furthermore, you must make a hit on your first time at bat, if you hope to stay in the game.

To play the game well, you will need to know the ground rules, the nature of the pitcher(s) you will face, and how the balls and strikes will be called. So let's look at the types and styles of interviews and interviewers, and how you will be scored.

HOW THE GAME IS PLAYED

The *screening interview* is the first type you are likely to encounter. It is your prospective employer's way of forming an initial impression of you—in dress, bearing, style, and attitude, among other things. If the first impression is favorable, the interview can move on to examine your basic qualifications, in terms of education, experience, and skills. Something in your résumé told the interviewer that there could be a matchup somewhere between your abilities and the needs of the organization. This must either be verified or discounted.

The screening interview will probably include a quick picture of the organization (and perhaps the specific position) you seek to enter, to determine your level of interest. Along this line, you may be asked about your reasons for leaving the service, for your choosing this particular career field, and for your choosing this particular firm. The screening interview does just what its name implies: it screens out applicants who are not fully qualified or not really interested.

In a *serial interview,* you will meet several interviewers in sequence, who will tell you more about the organization and the position while trying to determine more closely whether you meet their expectations. When it is necessary to cover more ground in a shorter time, a *group interview* might be scheduled instead, allowing you to meet several company representatives at the same time. In some cases, an informal group interview (e.g., lunch with several executives) may take place in addition to a serial interview.

All these interviews are two-way streets. The organization is seeking to meet its needs; you should be doing the same thing for yourself. Ask your own down-to-earth questions, even as you are answering theirs. In a structured interview, found most often during the initial screening process, their questions will usually follow a format that is designed to ferret out the most-frequent reasons for job candidates failing to qualify. A more normal interview goes beyond a format, and their questions can jump all over the lot. But so can yours. So keep your cool.

It's relatively rare these days, but if you are in the running for an extremely high-level or demanding position, you could encounter a *stress interview*—of the sort immortalized by the late Admiral Hyman Rickover, as he personally evaluated applicants for the Navy's nuclear-power program. In these, the interviewer assumes an adversary role, to test poise and motivation under pressure. In some cases, the pressure-cooker demands of the position truly may call for such an interview technique; in others, your potential boss simply may be a tyrant. If so, think again about how badly you might want to work for him.

What actually happens on game day depends on the size of the organization you seek to join, the level of position you're after, and the way you obtained the interview. So let's set up a hypothetical example: say, a medium- to large-size company, with a position somewhere between entry and mid level, and with an interview stemming directly from your résumé. In other words, let's imagine that you are coming in cold—with no connections to the company you might want to join.

First, you are likely to see an assistant from the personnel (or human resources) department. This will be the screening interview, highly formatted. Let's assume you pass—and they pass. Next, you will probably go to a supervisor or department manager, who will go into more depth about the position and what they would expect of you. Remember—they are trying to get a fix on your abilities; at the same time, you should be trying to get a fix on your own interest in the position.

So far, so good. We move to the next level—perhaps a director or vice-president this time. In addition to confirming a good fit, they will be looking for signs of your upward potential within the organization. Somewhere during this stage, you could find yourself in a group-interview situation. This second stage could stretch out a bit, depending upon the availability of company personnel and your own availability for interviews.

In a smaller organization, the process could be compressed, and you could be talking to the head of the firm by the second step of the interview process. The key point to remember is: Stay flexible; be ready for anything. The process could be stretched out, or you could have six interviews in one day—with a number of questions repeated six times. Just remember to regard each interview and each step as the most important one in the process, whether it be with the firm's president or a potential co-worker. Be assured that someone will be collecting and reporting all the comments and opinions that emerge during your interview process—and one strong negative remark can shoot you down.

Here's a real-life example: A major advertising agency flew a well-qualified candidate (let's call him Felix) to New York City for interviews. He arrived on a Monday and was scheduled for six interviews on Tuesday, capped by dinner with two agency executives Tuesday evening. If all went well, the candidate would receive an offer from the agency Wednesday morning, have lunch with a vice-president that noon, and be on his way home that afternoon to consider the offer.

The fifth interview on Tuesday was with a senior vice-president named Sam; the final stop of that marathon day was with a relatively junior member of the company, Ray. That evening's dinner was relaxed: two rounds of drinks beforehand, wine with dinner, and an after-dinner nightcap. Late in the evening, Felix was asked how his interview with Ray went.

"Oh, that was a waste of time," Felix said. "Ray asked me all the same questions that Sam did. And I had already hit it off pretty well with Sam."

The agency arranged an early flight home Wednesday morning

for Felix. "Thank you for coming, but we have had a sudden change in plans . . . "

Why? The agency concluded that the apparent lack of respect for Ray's opinions foretold possible conflicts with Felix's peers, as a result of the seeming shortfall in a team-player mind set. They also questioned whether this absence of tact would spill over into relationships with their clients. They also concluded that the "all was well with Sam" comment revealed too much unwarranted familiarity and presumption, much too early in the game.

As the agency's director of human resources finally remarked, "He had a good military background; he had the skills we could use. But we just couldn't take a chance on his poor interpersonal skills."

How can you avoid a similar fate? After all, "interpersonal skills" is such a vague term. What are prospective employers really looking for, anyway?

THE FIFTEEN CRITERIA

After surveying fifty small-, medium-, and large-size companies, I came to a conclusion that you should find comforting. Most civilian employers are looking for the same things that your reporting seniors were looking for, throughout your military career. So you are on familiar ground—just take a look at the composite interviewer's score sheet in Figure 8.

These fifteen criteria cover the waterfront. They showed up in virtually every company's evaluation sheet. This does not mean that all employers will look equally hard at all fifteen—they will look hardest at those meeting their specific needs—but sooner or later most of these will come into play.

At one of my Washington, D.C., seminars, representatives from all five uniformed services were in the group. One remarked that these fifteen criteria seemed to have come from his service's fitness reports. I asked for blank reports from all services, and the next

Figure 8. The Interviewers' Fifteen Criteria

Communication: Expresses ideas clearly in speech and writing.
Intelligence: Quickly grasps assignments; contributes new ideas.
Self-confidence: Shows maturity and poise in all situations.
Responsibility: Recognizes what needs doing and sees to it.
Initiative: A self-starter; takes action without being told to.
Leadership: Skillful at guiding and directing others.
Energy: Tireless; sets the pace for his co-workers.
Imagination: Can deal with nonroutine problems in original ways.
Flexibility: Receptive to new situations and ideas.
Self-knowledge: Recognizes own strengths and weaknesses.
Conflict Resolution: Handles stress and antagonism skillfully.
Competitive Spirit: Thinks and acts like a winner.
Achievement: Sets goals and attains them.
Education and Skills: Possesses the right combination for the job.
Sense of Purpose: Translates personal needs into long-range goals.

day we ran a check. The criteria were covered, in one way or another, on all five reports.

In addition to private industry and the armed services, government agencies—from local municipalities up through federal service—use variations of these criteria in evaluating their employees. So you will run into them practically everywhere you turn.

This is all to the good, because we have already been through this drill, when we conducted the self-inventory back in Chapter Two. Working back through duty assignments, you came up with lists of assets and liabilities, later encapsulating the assets in developing your résumé. Now's the time to bounce that list of your assets off these fifteen criteria, to come up with specific examples that you can draw upon during the interview.

Break out a pencil and paper, and take it from the top. For example:

COMMUNICATION

> Always marked excellent to outstanding in this area on fitness reports

❯ As assistant operations officer, commended for clarity and attention to detail in written operations plans and orders

❯ As battalion adjutant, revised and updated administrative orders and directives

❯ Selected as regimental command briefer for visiting dignitaries . . .

. . . and so on.

So when a prospective employer states, "An important part of this position is the requirement for strong communication skills," you should be locked and loaded—ready to fire away. Conversely, in areas where the employer's strongest needs do not match your strongest skills and attributes, you may be able to state with confidence, "I don't believe my background is as strong in that area as others, but here's what I did in a similar situation . . . " or, "I'm a quick study, and I think I can get up to speed rapidly in that function . . . "—but only if you've thought things through beforehand and are convinced that you are not making empty promises.

Working your way through these fifteen criteria should help you build all the self-assurance you need. I have hired people whose lack of specific skills was outweighed by self-confidence and a willingness to learn. These two key attributes come directly from self-knowledge and a positive attitude—world beaters, every time.

FIRST IMPRESSIONS: THE HALO EFFECT

There's one more thing you should know: Your interview—almost any interview—will consist of two parts. We have been working together to prepare you for the second part, in which you match the skills and attributes you have developed over the years against the requirements of your prospective employer. Your careful, sometimes painful preparation will pay dividends—but first, you must get that far!

It's the leadoff part of the interview that can kill you.

It is tied in with a phenomenon that psychologists call the "halo effect.'' You have seen it at work in school, in military service, and in other situations where an individual's display of proficiency in one area creates a presumption of proficiency in other areas— as in the case of the star quarterback who is automatically a front-runner for class president and the actor who plays a doctor on television testifying before Congress as an expert witness on health care.

During an interview, the halo effect has to do with the first impression you make on a prospective employer, and it can be positive or negative. Either way, it radiates in all directions from that initial picture you present. Research has shown that employers often make up their minds about job applicants in the first thirty seconds of an interview. Psychologist Joyce Brothers has labeled this the "thirty-second hurdle.'' If you fail to clear that hurdle, your chances of getting the job are quite slim, no matter how well you do in the rest of the interview. On the other hand, your ability to sail over that first hurdle may even cause the interviewer to give you more credit than you actually rate in later stages of the evaluation process.

Thinking about some of the talented men and women who have crashed and burned in the first thirty seconds, for reasons they could have controlled, still brings tears to my eyes. The thing is—every one of them realized it, almost immediately! If you blow it, you know it.

THE TACKY TEN

In the last chapter, I gave you a list of seven areas to examine, to help ensure a favorable first impression. During one seminar, a senior officer called such a list an insult to his intelligence. Maybe so—the list is almost painfully basic. But it is derived from mistakes that real people have made, and I hope you have given it some thought. As a final checklist to consider before stepping into the interview room, please consider these ten most egregious halo tarnishers:

> Being late for the interview
> Dressing inappropriately (one candidate for a six-figure job showed up in a leisure suit, to show he could be casual)
> Offering a limp, cold-fish handshake
> Making poor eye contact
> Making derogatory remarks about previous employer
> Chewing gum or smoking (one misguided applicant offered his prospective employer a Cuban cigar, to display his clout)
> Giving rambling answers with extraneous details
> Being unable to respond maturely, when asked for self-assessment of strengths and weaknesses
> Having no knowledge of the company or its products
> Asking questions that relate only to salary and benefits; nothing about the job itself.

Please keep the tacky ten in mind, as we examine them in more detail, inside the interview room.

THE DAY OF THE INTERVIEW

Whatever you do, get there early. If you're late, you're dead. If you just make it by the skin of your teeth, you will likely be distracted, perspiring, and otherwise showing lack of poise—and you're dead.

If you get there about fifteen minutes early, you'll have time for a quick personal preinspection (How many years have you been doing these?): hair in place; tie straight; jacket or dress free of loose hairs, threads, or flakes; shoes dust free; stockings run free (it's wise to have an extra pair of pantyhose in your purse, in case of emergency); glasses clean; breath mint handy (a good brush and floss within an hour of the interview is best, if you can swing it— but even *that* won't overcome the lingering effect of garlic the night before or onions the same day).

Don't let your initial handshake with your interviewer sabotage your first impression. A sweaty-palm handshake is a poor testimonial to your self-confidence. If necessary, make a last-minute restroom stop to wash your hands in hot water and dry them thoroughly—then give them a final wipe with a pocket handkerchief just before going through the interviewer's door. At the very least keep a handkerchief or tissue handy in pocket or purse.

Let the interviewer(s) make the first move in extending the greeting. Respond with a firm handshake (no bonecrusher, please) and *direct eye contact.* You may or may not be greeted by your first name. If so, do not return the familiarity unless and until you are specifically invited. (If first-naming is never made reciprocal, you might want to take a closer look at personal relationships within the firm before you sign on.)

If you stand around talking for a while, keep your hands out of your pockets. The interviewer would like to see you relax, but not become so casual that you trivialize the process. You may be asked to take a specific chair, but if you have a choice of sitting across from or beside an interviewer, take the seat beside, to eliminate invisible barriers and equalize the situation a bit. Some experts maintain that individuals tend to pay more attention to people and things on the left side of their field of vision than on the right side. So if you are asked to sit down across from the interviewer, why not play the odds and take a seat slightly to his or her left, if possible?

No matter where you wind up sitting, be certain to *maintain eye contact.* Looking your prospective employer squarely in the eye may not wrap up the job for you, but failure to do so can surely lose it for you. The interviewer will be less likely to chalk up an averted gaze to shyness (after a career as a military leader?) and more likely to attribute it to low self-esteem or unreliability. Or he may think you are trying to hide something.

This message about eye contact is crucial. It has been the downfall of too many good people. If you have *any* doubts about your abilities in this key area: practice, practice, and practice some more, until looking people in the eye becomes second nature. It's the only way to get across the thirty-second hurdle with confidence.

Having said that, I must caution against overcompensating with too riveting a gaze. Nobody likes to be stared at, and interviewers are just as sensitive to this as anyone else. So don't be afraid to break eye contact every once in a while—as long as you remember to go back.

THE REST OF THE INTERVIEW

You have made it past the first thirty seconds, and you are moving directly into deeper discussion. At this stage, remember that the company wants to find out all it can about you—to see if you will be able to help solve its problems and contribute to its profits. At the same time, you will want to learn all you can about the company's operations, strengths, and weaknesses—to see if your talents will match its needs. Will this company challenge you, give you room to grow, and help you fill your own needs? At some point the interviewer will probably describe in some detail the position the company is trying to fill. Feel free to make some brief notes and jot down questions as they occur to you. (I am always impressed by the seriousness of candidates who bring a note pad to the interview, and strongly recommend that you bring an eight-and-one-half-by-eleven or a five-by-seven-inch pad in a vinyl binder or folder, with a sleeve in which you can tuck some extra résumés, a fact sheet on the company, and a list of questions you will want to ask the interviewer [to be covered in Chapter Nine].) Just don't immerse yourself in note taking to the point where you lose the eye contact you've established. You don't need a word-for-word translation later on; a few key words to remind you of major points will suffice.

QUESTION TIME

Here is a sampling of questions you are likely to face. Study them, then write out your own answers in as much detail as possible. Before each interview, you should go back and polish your answers, making them more relevant to the company doing the interviewing.

You can bet you will be asked this question in one form or another, usually early in the interview:

"What can you tell me about yourself?"

This is not a cue to break out your baby pictures or launch into your high school triumphs back in Buffalo. The interviewer is looking for clues to your character, your motivation, and your ambitions—in other words, the things that make you tick. A possible answer could be:

"Ever since working as an auto mechanic in high school, I have had a thirst for troubleshooting. I'll work for hours to break down a problem and get to its roots. Over the years, I've earned a reputation as someone who can fix just about anything. I guess this persistence applies to all areas of my life. I finish every task I start, and the more challenging the better. I work hard to be the best at whatever I do."

An answer like this shows initiative, self-confidence, imagination, and a competitive spirit. It has the added value of being brief (try to keep your answers under a minute long, if possible). Concise answers that go to the heart of the questions show the interviewer that you have strong oral-communication skills. Long, rambling answers, on the other hand, tend to lose the questioners—and worse yet, bore them. Don't worry about failing to pack every possible bit of information into each answer. If interviewers want to learn still more about you, they will ask.

From this type of leadoff question—given a responsive answer—a skilled interviewer can move along, opening windows into your background, personality, self-knowledge, skills, and direction. Your job here is to make the interviewer's task easy, presenting a clear, detailed picture of yourself, with clean-cut edges—no fuzziness. You want your strongest qualities to stand out, while dealing with your weaker ones in ways that show your human side, as well as your clear self-knowledge and your determination to keep honing and improving your skills.

Here comes a typical window opener:

"How would you describe your personality?"

"As a kid, I was very confident—cocky, almost. I wasn't afraid of anything. I was very competitive and worked hard to excel at sports and school activities, but I didn't do as well in the classroom. I knew I had the ability, but I just didn't apply myself. When I was sixteen, my life turned around. I went to a church camp and learned to accept responsibility and set goals for myself. Somewhere along the way, I developed a sense of perseverence as I would get knocked flat on my face from time to time on the way to my various goals. As an adult, I've tried to maintain high standards for myself, while expecting my associates to do the same. As I became more senior in rank, I guess I developed an overly critical attitude toward my contemporaries and my subordinates who didn't meet my expectations, but this attitude took a one-hundred-and-eighty-degree turn when my commanding officer noticed it and landed on me with both feet. Once he saw that I had the message, he gave me a lot of support. That really showed me a lot. Since then, I have a better idea of the value of patience, and I'm a lot better at living with people's limitations while encouraging them to improve."

An answer like this shows a lot of self-knowledge and a willingness to correct weak areas. A competitive, goal-oriented individual who can accept responsibility shows through. And once again, this answer has the virtue of brevity, while covering a lot of ground.

You will probably be asked about your military service. There are several possible variations on this theme:

"Why did you go into the service?"

"A man I respect a great deal served in the Army during the Korean War. From time to time, he would talk about his experiences and recall how much he had matured in the Army. He said that many of his values and his strong sense of self-discipline came directly from his military training. At the time, I felt that I was lacking in maturity. I hoped that the Army would help me find a

sense of purpose and put my life on track, headed in a positive direction.''

or

''If you had it to do over again, would you still join the service?''

''Absolutely. I complained a lot at first, but after a while I realized that the Navy was offering me the structure and discipline I needed to reach the goals I was setting for my life. I was also given a lot of responsibility early on, far more than my buddies on the outside had.''

or still other variations

''What did you like most (or least) about your military career?''

or

''How did your spouse feel about the military life?''

Here comes the first curve ball. I hope you have done your homework and learned something about the company interviewing you, before you go after this potential strikeout pitch—so you don't carry on too enthusiastically about features of military life the company can never offer—or bad-mouth some aspects of military life that happen to be hallmarks of that company's way of doing business.

What *did* you like most? This is no time to play Rambo, unless you are applying for work as a hit man or soldier of fortune.

''The structure and discipline I encountered in the service have helped me become more organized and efficient over the years. I'm more organized now than I ever thought I could be. My infantry experience has helped me develop planning skills, considering all aspects of a complex problem and pulling together the resources needed to get the job done in the time allotted. But I guess my strongest feelings are the pride I will always have in my buddies, my unit, and my service—and the strong loyalty we will always feel for each other. We will never let each other down.''

Structure . . . discipline . . . planning skills . . . loyalty—a four-bagger in any league! Firms are always looking for team players. Now, what did you (and presumably your spouse) like *least?*

''Well, neither my wife nor I liked the periods of separation

*whenever I deployed overseas, but I think we made the most of it.
I tried to use my time away from the family for self-improvement
with correspondence courses, and she became much more self-
sufficient while I was gone. And, of course, the homecomings were
great—some of the happiest times of my life."*

It's usually best to stay upbeat, even when answering a negative
question. If the company plans to put you on the road a lot, and
that's precisely what your spouse detested about military life, the
interviewer may pounce on this as a source of trouble further down
the road and you need to preempt such a line of questioning. Of
course, if such a basic conflict truly exists, it's probably best for
all concerned to smoke it out early. We're talking about the rest of
your life (and your spouse's) here.

Finally, the big question:

"Why are you leaving the service?"

There's a spin on this one, too—but it's no trickier to handle
than a question directed to any other applicant about why he left
his last job. You might as well put your own positive spin on the
answer—that you are moving boldly into Phase II of your life,
rather than clinging to the security blanket of Phase I:

*"I wouldn't trade my military experience for anything, but it's
time to move on. I have another twenty good working years ahead
of me, and I am eager to get on with my second career."*

From time to time, the interviewer might toss you a change-of-
pace pitch, to check your resilience and sense of timing. Watch out
for this one, which has fooled many a fine batter:

*"If you could choose an ideal career, what and where would it
be?"*

If you blurt out something like "tennis pro in San Diego," you
logically might be asked why you are interviewing for a management information systems position in Norfolk. You'd better have a
good answer that stays within the ballpark:

*"I think I am already on the track of an ideal career for me. My
undergraduate degree is in computer science, and my career pattern in the Air Force has built upon that knowledge in a succession*

of assignments of increasing responsibility in the information sys-
tems field, together with postgraduate work. The position with your
firm is the next logical step, and I'm excited about it.''

Another seemingly innocuous, but loaded question is:

"Tell me about your interests, or how you spend your off-duty
hours.''

Your answer can give your interviewer a number of clues about
your personality, intellect, and drive. Unless you are planning to
become a television critic, an answer of "watching television, reading, and listening to classical music" might leave an impression of
a sedentary, noncompetitive individual with a low energy level.

On the other hand, more active pastimes such as tennis, mountain
climbing, antique-car restoration, or writing books and magazine
articles leave impressions of risk taking, stamina, imagination, and
intelligence. Volunteer work and religious activities that show compassion and a sincere interest in people reflect an important dimension of spiritual qualities.

As an interviewer, I look for balance. To me, an applicant who
is coming from or looking for a pressure-cooker job—and whose
off-duty pastimes lean toward demanding, high-energy avocations—is a candidate either for a heart attack or a breakdown. I am
just as wary of workaholics, who have no off-duty pastimes because
they never leave the office. They are potential head-hurters for any
organization.

Here's another tricky question:

"What was the biggest personal challenge you faced in your life
or in your career?''

Think about it. I have interviewed war heroes, professional ath-
letes, entertainers, and other public figures with riveting stories to
tell. In most cases, I believed their tales of glory. But most of these
stories were irrelevant to the needs of my boss, the head of the
employing company.

To show the boss why he should hire you, it may be more appropriate to recall the way you handled a personal or family crisis,
where strong moral fiber and depth of character were essential. This

may be the only place in the interview where you get a chance to display the skills you have acquired over long military service in resolving delicate, sensitive, or even life-threatening situations:

"Women comprise only ten percent of the armed forces, so it came as no great surprise when, on one tour of duty, I found myself as the only female on a headquarters staff of fourteen officers. That in itself is not tragic, but two officers on this small staff were determined to make my life miserable. They challenged me on almost every issue—big or small—especially when others were around to see.

"It was time for some mental toughness. To meet the challenge head-on, I had to do three things: become really competent in my job; keep my cool while under attack; and win over (or at least defuse) my two antagonists.

"Things began to move when one of my tormentors had to take emergency leave following the death of his mother. I sent him a brief sympathy note, recalling some of my feelings when my father passed away two years earlier. Meanwhile, I screwed up my courage and asked the other antagonist for advice on a major report I had to prepare. He agreed, and provided some extremely useful input. I sent him a packet of three quality golf balls with a note that said, 'Thanks for the lift you gave my report; I hope these will give your game a lift, too.'

"Before long, those two became my strongest supporters on the staff. I will never forget that turnaround."

THE HOME RUN BALL

Finally, to round out the interviewer's picture of your personal makeup, you are virtually guaranteed to get this question, in one form or another:

"What are your strongest qualities; what are your weakest? What are you doing to improve?"

Don't ever show up for an interview without having your answer to this one well thought out. There's nothing tricky about this pitch.

It floats up to the plate like a balloon ball, and you should be able to knock it out of the park. Here's one way of taking a cut at it:

"I am basically a hard charger—the kind of guy who will walk through a wall to carry out his assignment. At the same time, I'm a team player who can take pride in something less than a starring role in getting the job done. I tend to get totally involved whenever I get into something.

"I guess that my biggest shortcoming comes straight from my strength: my desire to do things right. At times, I have been too critical of my contemporaries and my subordinates when they have not seemed to measure up. I have learned the hard way that such criticism often succeeds only in making things worse, and have since learned how to take someone aside, explain what needs to be improved, and encourage the individual to do better. That has done wonders for my blood pressure, and it has become a matter of pride for me to see those I have trained move up the ladder. In fact, bringing along others to take my job has proved to be the best way of boosting myself up the ladder."

THE BACKGROUND QUESTIONS

After the interviewer decides that he has sized up your personal qualities, he will zero in on your work experience:

"What did you do in the service?"

You should treat this question and all other questions about your military assignments as though the interviewers have no knowledge of military service—including military jargon, which is likely to be totally foreign to them. If you cannot describe what you do in everyday English, they will not be able to relate your experience to the needs of their company.

If you spent your entire career in one specialty, this question is easy to answer, in thirty seconds or less: *"I was a supply (or procurement) specialist . . ."* then tell them what you actually did, stressing the elements of your work that would be of most interest to the company.

It is more likely that you have worked in more than one field. Your primary specialty may have been infantry, but over the course of a career you also may have been a recruiter, an instructor, a logistician, and a high-level planner, as well. This is where our opening drill of breaking each assignment into functions actually performed will prove especially valuable, enabling you to develop a list of skills you've acquired that will match the requirements of the job you seek.

If you are interviewing for a sales representative position, for instance, the employer may be most interested in your tour of recruiting duty, because it involves selling: generating leads, follow up, and closing. The instructor tour would also be of interest, in that it involves organizing large amounts of material and presenting it effectively. The planning experience, encompassing painstaking analysis of the past and present with foresightedness, adds to a very favorable picture of a top sales representative: organized, forehanded, persistent, a self-starter, a strong finisher . . . and so on.

In smaller firms, versatility and a willingness to do what has to be done are key attributes. Take the case of Tim, who was in a preliminary interview with the operations manager of a fifty-employee company when an emergency call came in. A combination of injury and illness had created a manpower shortage on the loading dock, and a critical deadline was at hand. While the operations manager started putting together a solution by telephone, Tim slipped out of the office, went to the loading dock, rolled up his sleeves, and pitched in. When the operations manager got to the dock, he saw Tim operating a fork lift, hoisting pallets onto a truck that had to roll.

Later, in his interview with the firm's president, Tim explained his actions: "In the service, I soon learned that you do what you have to do, to get the job done. The mission comes first."

Tim got the job—over six other applicants.

A natural follow-up to a what-did-you-do question would be:
"What was your proudest achievement in your career?"
It might have been receiving the Silver Star for heroism in com-

bat, but you have to keep your eye on the ball. Today, you are out gunning for that sales representative's job:

"As recruiters, we lived and died by the quotas we had to meet each month. I had to organize my time very carefully, because there was none to spare, even after working long hours for six days a week. After a while, I was able to build a strong and reliable network of people around town who could provide me with recruiting leads. I think I've always had an instinctive ability to size up people and what motivates them to do the things they do, so I particularly enjoyed the one-on-one contacts with prospective recruits. I never failed to make quota, and at the end of the tour, the hard work paid off in a citation and medal from my service and other recognition from the community that had become my own. I was most proud, though, of the success rate my enlistees achieved during recruit training. To me, it meant that I had picked them right, and had not misled them about what they were getting into."

The initial positive impression has been reinforced, most strongly. Now stand by for a big question:

"Have you ever been instrumental in reducing costs of your unit's operations? If so, how?"

Depending on the position and the level you seek, this type of question can make or break you. If you have done your homework, some good answers should appear in your self-evaluation work sheets and should be fresh in mind for the interview.

You needn't be a high-level operator to save money. Take the case of the staff sergeant on independent duty with a reserve unit, who had a hard time quantifying savings in the motor pool he ran. After we talked, we saw that:

> His switch from disposable wipe rags to discarded linens from local hotels and restaurants resulted in savings of fourteen hundred dollars per year.

> The checkout system he established saved some thirty-one hundred dollars in lost or missing tools during the first year.

> He reduced the downtime of vehicles awaiting maintenance by

more than 50 percent, by setting up a voluntary program for reservists to pull maintenance during the week, instead of waiting for weekend work.

You might encounter another shift of gears at this point:
"Please give me an example of your leadership style."
or
"Can you give me an example of your solving a problem by creative or innovative means?"
Some of your most vivid examples might come from your combat experience. Don't use them. Instead, state briefly your leadership philosophy:

"I believe in leading from the front. That doesn't mean a lot of wild yelling and arm waving, but it does mean being out where the troops can see you, and taking an interest in what they do without micromanaging. It means evenhandedness in administering awards and punishment, and it means setting clear-cut, attainable goals, ensuring that everyone understands the importance of meeting them, then getting out of the way and letting them try to surpass those goals. And they will, more often than not."

Then follow with an example of the way your subordinates made you proud of them by exceeding your expectations. By focusing your response on your troops and their accomplishments instead of yourself, you establish yourself as a results-oriented leader who really cares about his subordinates.

Innovative or creative problem solving is another facet of leadership that often involves finding a direct and obvious solution that has been overlooked at first. Examples:

❯The captain of an amphibious ship overheard one of his sailors referring to embarked Marines as "green parasites," and sensed that perhaps his crew did not understand the ship's mission fully. He had the sailor outfitted with a field uniform and equipment, and sent him ashore with the Marines for a physically demanding week-long exercise. The sailor returned dog tired, but excited and happy. By the time he finished telling his buddies about what really happened on the beach, his crew's understanding of the Marines and pride in their own mission had increased remarkably.

＞An Army captain volunteered to take over the dispirited music program of a suburban church adjacent to his base. The choir would number somewhere between six and ten each Sunday, making it impossible to plan a music program that could actually be sung on schedule. The captain's first announcement was that he would limit the size of the choir to thirty, until he got the ''sound'' he wanted. After that, new members would be accepted only after auditions. The choir was filled within two weeks, and on its way to an exciting season that culminated in their recording Handel's ''Messiah.''

＞A Marine general on Okinawa saw the potential for a morale problem after receiving a new mission: to offload tracked and wheeled vehicles from a squadron of maritime prepositioning ships and conduct preventive maintenance. Staying on top of his own maintenance requirements was onerous enough, without having to service vehicles that someone else would eventually use. But after he (truthfully) asserted that those who tackled these maintenance chores would be making Marine Corps history in carrying forward the new prepositioning concept, he had volunteers driving to the harbor from all over the island, sleeping in their vehicles as they awaited their turn to pull maintenance on someone else's tanks and trucks. The general was quick to admit that his action represented a new twist on an old ploy, used many years earlier by a boy named Tom Sawyer, who had to get a fence whitewashed.

The interviewer might try another test of your abilities at self-evaluation:

''What would your boss say about you?''

As the recipient of periodic fitness or efficiency reports, you *know* what your bosses have said about you, for the record. Your reported strengths and weaknesses should have emerged in recognizable patterns during your Chapter Two self-analysis. You should have a reasonable idea of the attributes the interviewer is seeking. So don't worry about describing yourself as a strong leader with sound analytical and planning skills and a good eye for detail, whose loyalty up and down the chain of command is unquestioned—if your boss(es) said it first.

The interviewer might want another reading on your interpersonal skills:

"Have you ever hired or fired anyone, or given anyone counseling? Please explain the circumstances."

Despite the fact that personnel turnover and personal counseling of subordinates are part of military life, some employers persist in believing that the armed forces—at all levels—deal harshly and arbitrarily with their people. This is your chance to show the interviewer that just isn't so.

"Counseling is mandatory every time I write a fitness report or other performance evaluation on one of my subordinates, and I have always tried to provide preliminary counseling, to ensure that those formal reports never came as a surprise to the one reported on. Since my responsibility for the welfare of my subordinates was near total, such counseling would go beyond the workplace, extending to such areas as financial management, conduct on liberty or leave, and marriage counseling. In complex cases, I was quick to refer my people to professionals.

"Actual hiring and firing in the armed forces is usually carried out by personnel and legal specialists at high command level, but officers and staff noncommissioned officers at all levels have the responsibility of making assignments and reassignments within their commands—to reward high-quality performance, to remove substandard performers, and to groom promising leaders for higher levels of responsibility. Going hand in hand with this responsibility is the need to provide adequate counseling about the need for the shifts. As a twenty-two-year-old lieutenant, I found myself in the position of having to provide much-needed counseling to a thirty-eight-year-old platoon sergeant. I had to proceed with tact, but without diluting the force of my convictions—and it worked! I have never been reluctant to counsel anyone since."

THE ULTIMATE QUESTION

This examination of your work experience may well come down to this final question:

"Why do you want this job?"

Such a simple question—but one that has tripped up many interviewees. The simple questions are the ones that nail you, especially if you haven't thought through your answers.

Well, why do you?

An adoption agency in Virginia had put a pair of prospective parents through three tough days of screening and interviews. The couple held up well, and near the end of the third day they and the social workers had finally begun to relax when one of the staff asked, quite casually, "Why do you want to adopt a baby?" The agency said later that this question is the most important one it asks, because it goes to the heart of an adopting couple's motivation. The answer it looks for is: "Because we love children." This couple passed the test.

So think about it. Why do you really want to work for this company? Is it because it is a leader in its industry? Is it because it has shown dynamic growth, and you sense that the chemistry is right for you to contribute to that growth? Is the reason that it has fallen on hard times and you think you can help because you believe in its product or service? Or is it something else?

If you want to get yourself crossed off its list, give the interviewer a Rio Grande response—a mile wide and an inch deep—such as:

"I think the job would be interesting."

or

"I'm a 'people' person." Ugh!

By the time you reach this point, you should know what attracts you to the firm, in rather specific terms. And if you feel that the interview has gone well enough that a job offer may be near, you *must* feel some excitement about the prospect. So say it—with feeling:

"I've always wanted to work for well-run organizations—whose names stand for quality—and I think I managed to do this for most of my military career. From what I've seen and heard here, I would be able to extend my winning streak. I am enthusiastic about the prospect of joining your team."

What more can anyone say?

Next, we will get into questions *you* can ask about the job.

9
....

NEGOTIATING THE JOB OFFER

A fter the interviewer finds out what he wants to know about your personality and your skills relative to the position he is seeking to fill, he may take time to tell you something about the company and the job. After a brief rundown, he will probably ask:

"What would you like to know about us?"

or

"Any questions?"

This is your time to shine.

YOUR TURN TO ASK

From this point on, you can set your own agenda. By asking the right questions, you can be sure that you understand correctly what the company is looking for, and you can put to rest any lingering doubts—in your mind or the interviewer's—about your suitability for the job. You should never leave an interview with any such doubts unresolved. Remember one of the key Laws of Murphy: In time, nature will reveal the hidden flaw—in any deal.

Here are some questions that most interviewers are prepared to field:

"What personal qualities would be ideal for this position?"

If by this time you have a good handle on the qualities the company is seeking and you see a good matchup, this question is a good way to set up a bit of personal horn tooting (with discretion, please) to remove any residual doubts the interviewer may still have. But remember this—something every good trial lawyer knows: *Never ask a question like this unless you are reasonably certain what the answer will be, and that the answer will be favorable in your case.* Getting blindsided by the interviewer at this point is just as disastrous as it would be for an attorney in a courtroom.

Another fair question (certainly as fair as the interviewer's "Why did you leave the service") you might ask is:

"Why is this position available?"

If the answer is, "The employee quit (or was fired)," you will want to find out why—once again proceeding with discretion. At this point, you can judge the veracity of the interviewer. If he hedges or retreats into vagueness, there might be a too-demanding boss or a too-heavy work load back in there somewhere. On the other hand, an answer like "The employee moved away (or became pregnant and left the work force)" is somewhat neutral, not revealing much about the job itself. Answers like "The person was promoted" or "It's a new position" are signs that real opportunity may exist there.

Once you're satisfied that you're not applying for a job nobody else wants, you will want to know more about your place in the company's pecking order:

"Where does this position fit on the organization chart?"

This, with good follow-up questions, should give you some idea of how the company's departments and divisions relate to each other. Are you joining the movers and shakers, or are they assigning you to the bureaucratic also-rans? Some small firms, of course, will not maintain an organization chart or any sort of wiring diagram— but you will still need to know who does what for whom.

Here are some related questions, as your understanding of departmental relationships improves:

"How does your performance-appraisal system work? How often will I be evaluated?"

"Who will be my reporting senior? What can you tell me about her?"

"Assuming I perform well, what kind of growth can I reasonably expect in this position?"

After exploring your own niche in the company, you can switch to more general questions:

"Where does the firm fit within the industry? Established leader? New, dynamic upstart?"

"Is the company pleased with its rate of growth?"

"Who provides the prime competition?"

"Who is the biggest customer?"

With these preliminary questions answered, you are now ready to edge toward more sensitive ground—both for you and the firm—by asking about turnover and company problem areas. A word of caution here: Individual firms do not work in a vacuum, so you must compare the performance of your firm against other firms in the same industry (and often the same region), rather than an unrealistic standard of perfection.

"What is the turnover rate here?"

By and large, a low turnover rate (say, 10 to 15 percent) says that the employees are generally happy where they are, for whatever reasons. Furthermore, companies with low turnover rates will usually be happy to do a little bragging about it. In fact, they might even raise the subject, if you don't. On the other hand, an "I don't know" or a vague answer with a high fog content must be probed, either during the interview or soon afterward. I repeat—you must keep in mind the big industry picture before rushing to judgment about an individual company. An industry-wide slump may have forced the company into layoffs against its wishes, and the very fact that it is hiring again could be a hopeful sign that far outweighs any raw statistics on turnover rates. You must keep things in context. Your task is not to sit in judgment of the company; your prime need is to discover how you and the company will match up, and whether you will be able to grow within it.

Along this line:

"What is the biggest problem the company is facing at present?"

Be careful with this one. If you have done your preinterview homework (and perhaps a bit of detective work, as well) you should have some idea of where problem areas exist (say, in marketplace exposure, safety record, training, or turnover). If you frame your question in a way that explores the possibility of applying new talent against one or more of the company's soft spots—and believe me, every company has them—you won't be perceived by the interviewer as a know-it-all bringing gratuitous criticism from the outside. Here's the point: Problems drain away profits—and if you can show how you tackled and solved similar problems during your military career, you might be worth your weight in platinum to a problem-ridden firm. Just remember: Don't be critical; instead, show concern and a desire to help.

Toward the end of your interview, try this question:

"Will I have a chance to meet some of the people I'll be working with?"

Sometimes, the firm will arrange for a lunch or another opportunity for you to meet your peers on a relatively informal basis. How nice. But this is not purely a social occasion. It is yet another opportunity for a two-way evaluation, in both a working and a social context.

If you are lucky, you may get a look at your immediate superior and immediate subordinate(s), as well. This could be vital. Here's why: Midlevel managers brought in from the outside sometimes find that some of their immediate subordinates are jealous and disgruntled, feeling that they should have been promoted before an outsider was recruited for the position. At the same time, the immediate superior may become fearful of being displaced by this new fair-haired wonder from the outside. To avoid such a no-win situation, be alert for danger signs—e.g., standoffish or openly hostile comments or body language—during the first encounter with these "old hands." You may be able to defuse things with an initial display of good-faith interest in them and the firm, as you express your desire to become part of the team. If not, you may wish to continue your line of questioning about the nature and severity of problems within the firm, and get your interviewer's take on the situation. If the answers are unsatisfactory, think twice about finalizing this deal.

Such competitive considerations aside, a few brief chats with current employees may reveal much about daily working conditions that might not otherwise emerge from an interview. They either can validate or undercut impressions you might have formed during your preinterview homework sessions, with former employees or even competitors.

Don't lose your nerve during this crucial phase of the interview, when the company has to answer *your* questions. Remember—there is no such thing as a base on balls in this deadly serious game. You must radiate confidence, saying in effect, "I have a lot to offer, and I am out to make the best possible fit." I never cease to be impressed with the candidates who ask me probing questions about the organization I represent—even with those who probe beyond my personal point of discomfort. I have usually found myself wanting to hire those who have been thorough (yet diplomatic) in their questioning, because they make me feel as though they would be faithful stewards of any assignment given to them. Seldom have they let me down.

ROUND TWO

Congratulations!

You have passed the screening interview and have been invited back for more talks.

They will tell you *when* and *where;* be sure to ask *with whom* and *for how long,* if they don't volunteer the information first. If the follow-up interview is scheduled to last an hour or longer, you can bet the questions will go into some depth; the field of contenders is narrowing and the competition is growing stiffer. What-ever the format, you must be even more alert and even better prepared than you were for the first round. The follow-up inter-views, conducted on the first or succeeding days, can present a number of surprises and new challenges.

Be prepared for luncheon or dinner sessions, aptitude testing, group interviews, or a visit with the corporation's "talking doctor" (staff psychologist). You might even be asked to attend a depart-mental meeting, to observe the company in operation. In fact, if you have revealed a pertinent problem-solving background in your screening interview, you might even be asked to take an active part in the meeting!

Here are a few points to remember, before you go into round two:

❯ Be sure to look over your notes and review the results of the screening interview at your first opportunity, while the meeting is still fresh in your memory. It should have given you a much clearer picture of your fit with the company than you had at the outset, and you will probably think of some questions you failed to ask during the first session. Conversely, you may also think of some questions they failed to ask you, which they certainly will ask later on.

❯ No matter how much good will and charm seem to pervade these follow-up interviews, *don't get too comfortable!* You are still on trial—under a magnifying glass, in fact—until you receive a job offer. The luncheon or dinner meetings will undoubtedly be friendly and relaxed, but getting too cozy at this stage has led to the down-fall of many an otherwise-qualified applicant, as we have seen ear-lier in Felix's case. Nurse your single drink or glass of wine with dinner, or stick to seltzer or coffee or tea if you have any doubts at all about your ability to remain sharp. This is no time to live on the edge. You're almost there—don't blow it.

❯ You may be asked, in a confidential and friendly way, to vol-unteer a critique or criticism of the company or one or more of its employees. This does *not* mean that you are on the team. They may be testing your knowledge of the company, your self-confidence, or your sense of tact and diplomatic skills. Be sensitive and circumspect—and above all, swallow any urge you may have to demonstrate your capacity for brutal frankness, lest you land with both feet on a raw nerve and find yourself out of contention.

Once again, you are not out of the woods until you receive a job offer. You still need to know how to transform the final stages of the interview into an offer you cannot refuse.

GETTING THE JOB OFFER

Up to this point, the company has called the shots. It has set the interview agenda and guided you through follow-up sessions. It has asked most of the questions, allowing you the opportunity to respond with your own questions after it gained the information it sought. It follows, then, that once you've cleared the interview hurdles you should be able to sit back and await the inevitable job offer.

Wrong!

More often than not, you will have to take charge of the interview process at some point, and subtly—or not so subtly—nudge it toward the job offer. But wait! After all my cautionary comments about overstepping your bounds, isn't this the worst form of overreaching?

Not this time. There are two reasons why:

❯ You have progressed past the personnel specialists, and now are engaged with the company's top management. Most of these decision makers are not professional interviewers. Their forte is in the professional disciplines: finance, data processing, or marketing, for example. Consequently, their ways of eliciting information about the applicant may be relatively unfocused and less likely than the earlier interviews to bring out the best the job seeker has to offer. So don't wait to be asked. You are too close to acceptance. You should be taking every opportunity to market yourself to your prospective employer.

❯The halo effect still applies here, and the decision maker may have formed his own subjective opinion of you in the first thirty seconds of your meeting. If he has reached a tentative decision and it is negative, he may cease to seek additional information, not wishing to be bothered by facts after making up his mind. You may perceive a noticeable loss of interest and drop in the energy level of this final interviewer, as your job-search effort grinds toward a perfunctory and unsatisfactory conclusion.

At this point, your internal RED ALERT indicator should be flashing wildly. If you are interviewing for a job you really want and see things starting to come unglued this way, it's time for crisis action. You've come too far to be counted out on strikes, with the bat resting on your shoulder. At this point, what do you have to lose by taking one last healthy cut at the ball?

Here's a personal example:

I was in Chicago, interviewing prospects for a regional sales manager's position. The field had been narrowed to three strong candidates, but a fourth had been added at the last minute. In terms of experience, Bruce didn't measure up to the other three, but something in his résumé had caught my attention and I had seen another spark during the first round of interviews. Bruce had twelve years' Air Force service, and had held his first civilian job for slightly more than a year. Unfortunately for him, I was looking for someone with seven to ten years' experience who had proven sales and sales-management skills.

Bruce had his act together. He presented a sharp appearance, a high energy level, and infectuous enthusiasm. He appeared to have his life under control, with a clear understanding of his capabilities and his shortcomings. He knew where he wanted to go in life. I had no doubt that with a few years' seasoning he could have handled that regional manager's job with ease.

I really struggled with this dilemma, but just could not get past Bruce's lack of sales and management experience. Finally, I told him so. He looked me in the eye and said, ''I know I don't have the experience you are looking for, and I understand your need to hire the best-qualified individual for the position. On the other hand, I've held some responsible assignments and attained high-quality results in the Air Force (he then gave a forty-five-second recap, emphasizing the talents he could bring to our company). I know quite a bit about your company (as he had amply demonstrated in two prior interviews), and it's just the type of organization I want to join. I may lack the product knowledge and the hands-on experience you are looking for, but I know I can produce the results you want. I am willing to start work for you in a lesser job at the same salary I'm making now (that was a real bargain for my company), and I will work my tail off to show you that I can produce.''

The sales manager's job went to one of the three experienced candidates. But I hired Bruce, too—as a sales representative. He kept his word, and produced the results he had promised. Five months later, another division of my company had an opening for a sales manager. I recommended Bruce and he won the promotion.

Sincerity, persistence, and guts can shine through when they are most needed, if you will let them.

WHEN DOES NO REALLY MEAN NO?

It's time to talk about growing a new skin—shedding the thin skin you've worn for a lifetime and growing a new one that can withstand the rigors of a long, strenuous job search. You may think you have a pretty tough hide already, but the chances are that your setbacks in even a moderately successful military career—much less a successful one—have been relatively few and far between. From time to time, you may have failed to receive orders for a desirable duty station or choice assignment, but chances are that most military professionals do not feel the first deep sting of rejection until the first time they get bitten by a selection board—during screening for promotion, for command or major school assignments, or most recently for retention on active duty.

A serious job campaign, on the other hand, is studded with turndowns. If you've never been through one before, you can't imagine how many ways people can say no. Keep in mind, however, that the reasons for rejection do not always relate directly to the applicant; sometimes, that's just the way things are. That's the bad news.

The good news is that there need be only one solitary yes at the end of the job-search trail to make everything okay.

This is where persistence comes in. Too many applicants regard a letter of rejection as the final word. In reality, however, it is not uncommon for companies to change their minds after the rejection letters have gone out. In many cases, it is possible for an applicant to get the ball rolling again.

Rejection letters almost always state that another applicant got the job. This is not always the case, however. Sometimes, for example, the company is ready to hire someone else at the time the letters are sent, but the deal is never consumated for one reason or another. In other cases, companies may be hazy about their job requirements and reject all applicants, after failing to hear any bells go off during the initial interview process. Then with the position still unfilled, they may decide to hire the next applicant who reasonably fits the bill. Still other companies may know the attributes of their ideal applicant, but at some point in the selection process they come to realize that such a perfect mortal does not exist, at least in their neck of the woods. Then they adjust their expectations and the next reasonably qualified person to show up gets the job.

In each of these cases, a rejected applicant can be reconsidered for the position, but the companies will seldom, if ever, reinstitute contact with anyone they've sent a rejection letter. So the applicant must take the initiative.

There are two ways you can tell that a rejection may be reversible:

❯The employer was sufficiently impressed with you to invite you back for a follow-up interview; and

❯You received the rejection letter shortly after the follow-up interview. The briefer that interval, the less likely it is that the employer has made an offer to and received an acceptance from another party.

If such is the case, you should respond to the rejection letter, restating why you were impressed with the company and reiterating why you still believe that you are the right person for the job.

If the company has not responded to your follow-up letter in two weeks or so, go ahead and call their personnel department to see if the job is still unfilled. If it is still open, you can then restate your interest—being candid, but not insistent to the point of turning off your listener.

Who knows? Sometimes the timing will be perfect, and you will have a job. And if it doesn't work, you're none the worse for having tried again. If you do find that someone else has been hired and the final answer is indeed No, don't give up. You still have two shots left:

❯Call or write the appropriate interviewers and company officials, thanking them for their consideration and expressing your interest in any similar positions that might open in the future.

❯Ask your interviewers to recommend other firms where your talents might be used. This moves you up another square in the networking game, and if the company was truly impressed by you but saw no chance of hiring you themselves, they just might give you a lead or a favorable endorsement.

NEGOTIATING YOUR SALARY

Any firm you seek employment with will try to hire you for as little money as possible.

That's right—they will try to get you on the cheap. But don't take it personally. In business, the bottom line is the bottom line, and keeping payrolls trimmed is part of the constant budget battle.

In almost any medium- to large-size organization, your position will have a salary range: entry level to midpoint to high end. Some firms may have a flat starting point for each position—take it or leave it. Others may give you some room to negotiate for a starting salary, but they will make every effort to land you in the entry-to-midpoint range, to allow for proportionately larger increases in salary as your performance improves with experience.

The question of salary could arise at any time during the interview process, but it most often comes up toward the end. From your standpoint, later usually is better, because that gives you more time to convince the company that you are the one it really wants. Ideally, you will know quite a bit about the company by the time a salary offer is made, and it will have a reasonably clear idea of the benefits it would reap if you joined them. If it wants you badly enough, the chances are good that salary negotiations will end favorably for you.

Even before you begin the interview process, it is absolutely essential to determine your basic salary *requirement,* below which you cannot dip in accepting a job offer. Consider all sources of income: military retirement pay and benefits, spousal income, investments, trusts, and all the rest. Balance that against your current or projected standard of living: mortgage, college expenses for your children, and all other life-style costs. The resulting gap is your rock-bottom figure. You may seek a higher salary, of course, but you can never go lower, no matter how attractive the position. Don't make a fool of yourself by going to an interview for a thirty-five-thousand-dollars-a-year position when you know that you cannot get by on less than forty thousand dollars. Charity is supposed to begin at home; it never begins in the marketplace.

Your prospective employer will bring up the matter of salary in one of two ways:

➤ "This position pays $_____ (or a range of $_____ to $_____)."

or

➤ "What salary are you looking for?"

At this point, you'd better have a good sense of what you are worth to your prospective employer. This has little to do with your own feelings of self-worth, or your overall value as a human being. You might be the world's greatest squadron commander or troubleshooter or parent or Scout leader or Sunday School teacher—

but in the marketplace the sum of your talents and potential services has a finite value, actual or perceived, that ultimately will be determined by the firm endeavoring to purchase it.

For example, if you desire a new career in education, and accept a position as a history teacher in the Seattle public-school system, your pay will be based on your teaching credentials. If you have a Bachelor of Arts degree in history, you will receive a salary scaled to a B.A. with no prior teaching experience. If you can demonstrate unusual experience or ability in the field (perhaps you have written one or more history texts or have written for historical magazines), you may receive extra consideration. Some school districts may factor in your military experience and move you up a bit on the pay ladder—but don't count on such a windfall everywhere you apply.

The same holds true for the data processing, electronics, and accounting fields, and many others besides. If you have the skills and can demonstrate a certain level of experience in your sought-after profession, you will receive pay commensurate with others at your level. Once you have taken hold of the job, you can advance more rapidly than your peers if you display the requisite talent and growth through positive contributions to your firm.

Let's set up a hypothetical example: You are a career combat-arms (infantry, artillery, or armor) officer who has amassed extensive line and staff experience and completed several tours of independent duty (recruiting, reserve training), as well. You have impressed your interviewers as being highly intelligent, self-confident, and articulate. You have shown enthusiasm and a high energy level, plus a capacity for handling conflicts, preferring to meet them head-on and resolve them with sound judgment, rather than shying away from them. You have no directly transferrable skills (say, in data processing or accounting). You are interested in city- or municipal-management opportunities, as well as midlevel management in small manufacturing firms. You are attracted to the way of life in medium-size Southern cities (preferably Greensboro, North Carolina, where you were raised).

With this kind of background, how do you go about determining what you should be seeking in a salary?

For openers, let's zero in on the field of city management. Your first step would be to seek out the appropriate trade association, both to determine where openings exist and to make contact with established figures in the field. Calls or letters to several of these people, explaining something about yourself and your status and asking for a bit of their time and counsel, will almost always get you started—at least to the point of understanding salary ranges and possibly to the point of obtaining specific points of contact for future employment opportunities.

The same technique applies in the search for an appropriate manufacturing firm. A visit to the head of the local Chamber of Commerce can provide substantial information—and even some direct contacts—in addition to the salary information you seek. In either case, you can begin the interview process armed with a realistic salary expectation.

We all have heard tales of the retirees from military service who have stepped directly into cushy jobs paying big bucks. Some of these stories may even be true. But by far the more common experience is to encounter an employer who is unwilling to pay for your lack of knowledge about his business, no matter what admirable qualities you may possess otherwise. A major factor in determining your initial worth to an organization is how much you must learn to become useful (and how long that will take). That's only fair, isn't it? Just turn the situation around: A well-known captain of industry—say, a Lee Iacocca—might have many of the qualities required of a great general, but no armed service would place him directly in command of an infantry division, or a numbered air force, or even a single ship. Why? Because he lacks the necessary experience, which is acquired in lower-level command and staff assignments.

Making an early determination of your true worth to a hiring company is especially important to a military retiree. Interviewers and vice-presidents can read military pay tables, which are in the public domain, and can calculate how much retired pay you are drawing. But that retirement pay is *your* earned income—not the hiring firm's. They have no more right to factor that into your starting salary than they would have to use your spouse's salary or your income from Aunt Emma's trust fund to artificially lower your compensation. It is one thing to start at the low point of a salary range because of a lack of prior experience; it is another totally unacceptable thing to start below the appropriate salary range altogether. Think ahead: If a firm will try to pull a stunt like that on you at the outset of your relationship, what will it try later on?

Conversely, if your salary demand is well above the current scale, the firm may legitimately ask why you feel you are worth that figure. If you don't have a convincing answer, based on hard evidence, you may have fouled that particular nest—permanently. Be sure to do your homework with respect to competitive salaries, and you won't have to deal with potentially terminal questions like that.

THE OFFER

"Bill, we feel you have the experience and talents we are looking for. We are prepared to make an offer of $_____. If this is acceptable, please let us know when you will be available to start."

"I appreciate your offer and your confidence in me, Mrs. O'Neill. How soon will you need a decision?"

You have an offer in hand. It is normal business practice to allow you a reasonable period of time to consider the offer. But what is reasonable? That will usually depend upon how badly you are needed. There might be a training class starting up that you need to attend. The firm may need help in meeting a major deadline of one sort or another, or solving a major problem. Whatever its needs, your own availability is another key factor. You might have to arrange a move, or perhaps you are waiting to hear from another company. In any event, you are not out of line in asking to take the offer home to examine it.

Take a good look:

> Does this job get you excited?
> Do you see an opportunity for growth?
> Is the starting salary within your acceptable range?
> What about the benefits package?

This is my first mention of benefits, and I've held off for a reason. Up to this point, the question of benefits should not have clouded your sense of the real issues—what you can bring to the firm and what the firm can do for you. But let's assume the initial salary offer is in the ballpark, and set it aside for the time being. It's time to look at the extras.

When you leave military service, many of the extras you took for granted will stay back on the base. There's a shock factor in having to pay for medical insurance or foot a dentist's bill for the first time in your adult life. And now you must also protect yourself against the catastrophic accident or the illness that puts you out of work for six months or longer—and disability insurance is expensive. If you're a retiree, of course, you can lay claim to some health-care benefits—*if* you happen to live near enough to a military hospital or clinic. But get in line. Your priority for treatment is below that of all active-duty military personnel and their families, *if* there's any time or space left by then.

In your initial calculation of bottom-line salary needs, you should have included the full list of military benefits that you now must cover out of pocket. Often, your new employer will cover some of these. But few, if any, will ever match the generosity of Uncle Sam.

If you are joining a large company, it may turn you over to a benefits specialist, who will give you a brochure that explains its package in great detail. Smaller firms may have a typewritten sheet or two. Take time to study all such material. Take nothing at face value, especially when dealing with smaller firms. They may say "Yes, we have a medical insurance plan"—but you may have to pay for it.

Let's take a closer look at some of the benefits that may be made available, and some of the questions you should be asking about them:

Medical Benefits

> Does the company pay all costs, or do you contribute?
> Are your family members included? Who pays for them?
> How much is deductible, and who pays that?
> Is psychiatric care included?
> Is vision care (including glasses) covered for you and your family?
> Does a dental-care plan, if there is one, cover both you and your family? How much is deductible? What are maximum benefits paid per year?
> Is orthodontic work covered? (This could be a big one, if you have a house full of kids who have inherited your overbite.)

It is very important to reach an understanding about preexisting medical conditions. If you or a member of your family is under treatment for a long-term illness, that either may not be covered by your new company's policy, or you may face a waiting period. Even without a preexisting condition, you may face a thirty-, sixty-, or even ninety-day waiting period under some setups, instead of being covered on the first day of employment. If conditions are otherwise satisfactory, you may have to cover this waiting period with a temporary policy.

Medical insurance costs are skyrocketing, so be sure to examine that benefits package carefully to determine everything you could be paying for and the ultimate impact of medical costs on your bottom-line salary needs. Be conservative in your estimates, because companies are sometimes forced by rising insurance costs either to reduce medical coverage or to call for a larger employee contribution to maintain the same level of coverage.

Disability and Sick Leave

> How many days of sick leave do you accrue each year? Can these be accumulated over the years?
> Do you have both short- and long-term disability coverage? Who pays for it?

Company Travel

> If you travel on company business, are you reimbursed for your actual expenses or on a per-diem basis? If the latter is true, what is the per-diem rate?
> How quickly are your travel expenses reimbursed? (This might seem like a throwaway question, but some smaller firms that operate close to the margin have been known to keep their employees waiting for months.)

Bonuses and Commissions

> Does the company pay bonuses for exceptional performance? When are they awarded?
> How about bonuses for beneficial suggestions, which result in cost savings or enhanced profits for the company?
> How are sales commissions and other incentives earned? When are they paid?

Training and Education

> How does the company train its employees for positions of increased responsibility?

> Is there a tuition-reimbursement program for work-related courses at local schools?

Miscellaneous

> If the company asks me to move, what expenses does it cover? Will it help me sell my house and find a new one?
> Is there a retirement plan? Does the company contribute? How soon will I be "vested" (eligible to receive benefits)?
> How is paid-vacation time earned? Can it be carried over from year to year? Can provisions be made for unpaid leave of absence under special circumstances?
> Is compensatory time given for overtime or weekend work?
> Does the company have a management-incentive plan?
> What other incentives does the company offer employees? Does it contribute to employee savings plans? Does it help defray the cost of home computers or other pieces of equipment that enhance employee proficiency on the job?

A FINAL CHECK

Okay. You've seen the salary offer and the benefits package. The money is right, and the company touches just about all the bases with its incentives and benefits. So you're all set to marry the firm and live happily ever after.

Or are you?

It's time to take one more good look at the total picture—at all aspects of this impending union. I tend to be impulsive at times, and I have fallen into the infatuation trap more than once during my career in business—and have deeply regretted it every time. To keep from marching off in the wrong direction to the wrong drummer, you could use one last check by a good devil's advocate, one who understands you and your needs clearly and who can discover the hidden flaws (if any) in the decision you are about to make. (If you are married, who could be better than your own partner? This is truly a joint decision, isn't it?)

At this point, you must make your strongest effort to "read" the corporation, to be certain that your abilities and goals mesh well with its way of doing business. Developing such a skill is essential for anyone who aspires to be a top achiever. It is a continual, life-long process of gathering, sorting, and evaluating the bits of information that, when assembled, will tell you if the corporate marriage you contemplate is really the one for you. Listen to that little voice inside. If it tells you that something isn't quite right, keep digging for more information to confirm or discount that feeling. Then act in your own best interest.

One brief example: One retired senior officer liked the package a major Defense contractor's Washington, D.C., office offered him. After some checking around, however, he realized that the firm (and others like it) made a practice of firing their military retirees within a few years, after their active-duty contacts at the Pentagon were either retired or transferred. He set out to study the corporation, looking for ways he could make himself valuable on a permanent basis. In time, he discovered a corporate deficiency in medium-range planning, which happened to be one of the strengths he had acquired during his military career. He sold both the need and his ability to fill it to the firm, and is now a senior vice-president.

NEGOTIATIONS: THE END GAME

You have made your final sanity check, and have decided that you want to work for the corporation that made you the offer. Your talents will be recognized and well used there. You have a real interest in the work, there is plenty of room for growth, and the chemistry seems right. The benefits package is outstanding—but let's say for the sake of argument that the opening salary it offers is a bit under your own financial bottom line. If you accept the offer, you'll be stretched too thin. This calls for negotiation.

Discussing money matters—especially your own—can be scary, embarrassing, painful, or all of the above. Wouldn't it be great to call for a pinch hitter right about now? To have a fast-talking agent or silver-tongued attorney step in to close the deal for you? But the cat's on your back. This is your final test. And you'll have to pass it on your own.

You must enter this final negotiation with the proper perspective. It is not a zero-sum contest, in which every gain for one side means a corresponding loss for the other. If this one is done right, both sides should emerge as winners. Let's look at it: You have the ability to contribute to the future success of your new employer. On the other hand, he provides the playing field and the opportunity for you to perform. You need each other, to make things work. So you should be entering the final talk in a spirit of filling each other's needs.

Let's look at the employer's needs first. He has an obligation to keep costs down and make a profit. Paying you more may or may not throw his budget out of whack—you probably can't tell at this stage. He is also gambling a little on your potential contribution, because you have no direct work experience in his field. On the other hand, his experience with other former military men and women tells him that you will be a loyal and productive employee, and he certainly needs more workers like that.

Now, let's look at your needs. You don't have enough breathing room. To accept this position, you might have to take on an additional job for a while (until your first substantial-enough salary increase), or draw down on your savings. Neither of these options should be appealing to any employer worth his salt. He really doesn't want your energies diluted, either by serving two masters or by living on the margin for any length of time.

Since you will be the one asking for something, it is up to you to come up with a plan, a win-win scheme that fills both your needs. Your approach might be something like this:

"Thank you again for the offer to join your firm. I'm excited by the prospect of contributing to a company like yours. I've taken a long look at your salary-and-benefits package, and matched it

*against my current financial obligations. It is very tight. I have looked at ways to reduce my own expenses, but it is still tighter than I can afford. If you could raise the offer by $*_____(be careful to give yourself a ten to fifteen percent cushion, in the event of a counteroffer) *I am prepared to accept the position right now and begin work on*_____.*"*

That is a sincere, straightforward approach. You have shown enthusiasm about the opportunity to contribute and you have stated your needs concisely and directly. You are not playing from weakness or emotion. If the organization can afford the salary adjustment, this approach will generally work.

But sometimes the firm cannot afford it:

"We appreciate your position, but our own budget is tight, and it will not allow us to bring you on board for any additional money at this time."

Then you might make your own counteroffer:

"Is there any way I can take on additional responsibilities in order to earn the income I need? Perhaps working overtime or on Saturdays?"

Or you might try this approach:

"I really want to work for you. I'll tighten my belt another notch and accept your offer if you will agree to give me a performance review in three months. That way, you will be able to see whether I will be worth the additional salary (go ahead and suggest a salary range, then ask the employer to set some specific, realistic goals for that trial period).*"*

Both of these approaches show a strong willingness on your part to walk the extra mile. Neither is adversarial, and neither deals in personalities or company policies. Each deals strictly with genuine needs—yours and the company's.

Approaches like these are recommended by most negotiating experts, and I personally have seen them work successfully many times in real estate transactions and other business deals, in addition to employment negotiations. The win-win approach is even a good way to set about settling family disputes.

Despite the overall success of this negotiating approach, it doesn't work every time. The company may be unwilling or unable to meet your counteroffer. In the final analysis, it all comes down to this: *How much do you want the job?* Are you willing to eat beans for a year to land the job of your dreams?

WALK AWAY LIKE A WINNER

If you decide to decline the offer, be sure to do it in style:

"Thank you for trying to work with me, but I must decline your offer with regret, because the salary would not enable me to make ends meet."

Follow this up with a nice letter. Don't burn your bridges with the company. Something else might open up, just down the road.

On the other hand, let's say the deal has been closed. You have a new employer and you feel terrific. There are still some things to do, though. It's time to break out some good stationery and write some thank-you notes:

❯First, a letter of acceptance and thanks to your new employer. If you won't be starting your new job immediately, keep in touch to show your continued interest, and ask about background materials you could be studying before you report for work.

❯Thank-you notes should go to everyone who has helped you in the job search. You can never send too many. Let them know where you will be and what you will be doing. Include a three-by-five card (for easy filing) with your new home and work addresses and phone numbers. You also can include a filled-out index card for contacts you expect to use soon. People don't forget thank-you notes.

It's a small world out there, and you'll never know when you will have to tap into your network again. You may think you have found the ideal job for life, but the uncertainties of the marketplace could always put you back on the street with little or no warning.

Remember—statistics say that you could be looking for another job in two to five years. So keep your eyes open.

10

LOOKING BACK...
LOOKING AHEAD

We have covered a lot of ground together. Keying on the stirring example set by George and Susan in turning around their lives, we have gone through an exhaustive process of self-inventory and prioritizing of needs and wants, as prelude to a systematic search process for an interest-driven second career. Keep in mind that George and Susan are real people. The other examples used in this book come from the experiences of real people, as well. If experience is indeed the best teacher, I hope that you will be able to benefit from their encounters—both good and bad—with the realities of the job search. Why learn from your own mistakes, when you can learn much less painfully from the missteps of others?

I cannot overstress the importance of the self-inventory process, in all its aspects. It is absolutely essential in getting you started in the right direction, in building your résumés, and in carrying you through the interview and final salary negotiations. A good salesman must know his product thoroughly—and in this case you are the product. From long experience on the other side of that interview table, let me state it flatly: The recruiters *know* when someone is winging it. Conversely, they are quick to recognize those who are confident in their self-knowledge. They are cleaner cut, with sharper edges. There is little doubt about who they are, what they want, and what they can do for the hiring company.

If you are tempted to shortcut your way through this vital process of self-examination, remember the case of the major who still thought he was a born administrator after three unsuccessful shots at it in CivLand. He did not turn things around until he put himself through a self-analysis process that proved he was on the wrong track. Old myths die hard—especially self-perpetuating ones. But die they must if you are to get on with life.

For some of you, the transition to Phase II will be just one more tricky mine field to get across. For others, it may well be the fight of your life, requiring intense soul-searching and major change. Your inability to control your new environment may lead to an entry shock similar to that experienced by a young Marine on his first day in Vietnam. When incoming mortar rounds started landing nearby, he jumped into the nearest foxhole, landing on top of a gunnery sergeant.

"Gunny—they're shooting at us!"

"That's okay, lad—they're authorized to."

Even though you do all the right things in preparing for the job search, you still may enounter a string of rejections unlike anything you've ever experienced, before you hear the one big yes that makes the hurt go away. Don't take the rejections personally. They're authorized. That's the way things are.

You might not be able to control your operating environment, but you weren't able to do that in combat or in other complex military evolutions, either. What you can control is your attitude and the way you handle yourself in times of difficulty.

In the Introduction, I listed the shared personal traits and characteristics of successful Americans—from all walks of life—who had prior military service. Virtually every one of you has all those traits—or at least the seeds of them—and all of them are within reach. Winding up that list were the admirable characteristics of steadiness under pressure and perseverance, hallmark qualities of military service. Now is the time to reach back and call on them once again.

Press on!

RESOURCE DIRECTORY

I have tried to pack into this book the experience and wisdom of many people and organizations, but no single source can tell you everything you will need to know to seek out, explore, and enter the interest-driven career field that will be the right one for you. Here are some additional sources of information:

Veterans Assistance. The membership fees are small and the benefits are enormous—e.g., job-seekers' workshops, job fairs, and a nationwide résumé-referral service, in addition to monthly magazines loaded with information about employment prospects—if you join one of these powerhouse organizations:

› The Retired Officers Association (TROA)
  201 North Washington Street
  Alexandria, Virginia 22134-2529
  (703) 549–2311 (800) 245–8762
› Non Commissioned Officers Association (NCOA)
  P.O. Box 33610
  San Antonio, Texas 78233
  (512) 653–6161

Determining Your Interests. The Strong Interest Inventory is a 325-item questionnaire that will help you determine your relative degrees of interest in a wide range of occupations, hobbies, leisure

activities, types of people, and even fields of study. A career counselor will find your inventory profile a valuable tool, but the results
are generally self-explanatory if you don't have the services of a
counselor. The Strong Interest Inventory is available at family service centers on most military bases, and at career development and
placement centers at colleges and universities. It is distributed by:

Consulting Psychologists Press
577 College Avenue
Palo Alto, California 94306

Image, Color, and Style. For a number of years, I have relied on
image consultant Robyn Winters, who speaks and conducts workshops on image, balance, and self-esteem throughout the country.
She may be reached at 2700U Bedford Street, Stamford, Connecticut 06905. Telephone: (203) 964–9551.

There are many books about this. I have found three to be particularly useful:

Color Me Beautiful by Carole Jackson (Ballantine)
Color for Men by Carole Jackson (Ballantine)
The Professional Image by Susan Bixler (Perigee)

Stress Management. Courses are offered through community colleges, churches, adult education programs, and Veterans hospitals.
Two useful books are:

The Relaxation Response by Herbert Benson, M.D. (Avon)
Stress Without Distress by Hans Selye, M.D.

(New American Library)

Federal Service. If you have been caught in the Department of
Defense downsizing crunch some years shy of qualifying for military retirement, you might want to seek career stability and retirement security on the government's civilian side, letting your years
of military service count toward full Federal retirement. Despite all
the talk of hiring freezes, there are plenty of moves to be made.

Nobody shuts down "the Feds." With more than three million employees and an annual turnover rate of about 10%, about 300,000 jobs are being filled each year. The key to Federal employment is the SF-171 form, which has replaced most of the old Civil Service Examinations and has the legal status of a written examination itself even though it is a detailed résumé, not a test. According to Gabe Heilig, president of the only company authorized to offer SF-171 and résumé services at the Pentagon, the trick in preparing the 171 form is to present more information—much more—than the application requests. But hard-nosed Federal screening panels are looking for *evidence* of your employability, expressed in *facts* and *plain English*—not a fantasy piece loaded with bullroar and buzzwords. For information and assistance, call or write:

Action Résumés
P.O. 46569, The Pentagon
Washington, D.C. 20050
(703) 979–8203 FAX: (703) 979–8204

General References. Let us begin with the networkers' dream:

Encyclopedia of Associations (Third Volume) (Gale Research Company) This lists more than twenty-two thousand organizations of all types and purposes, including public service, military and veterans, cultural, patriotic, and scientific associations. It even includes fraternities, sororities, and fan clubs. Membership is described in terms of organizational goals and individual criteria, size and location of chapters, and major activities, and includes a four-year convention schedule where appropriate. Addresses, telephone numbers, and points of contact are listed. This reference is particularly useful in helping you locate placement committees, which can tell you of specific job openings in your fields of interest. By contacting listed organizations, you also may be able to obtain membership lists as a means of developing a network of personal contacts in your field.

Bureau of Labor Statistics Publications. The Bureau of Labor Statistics (BLS) publishes a comprehensive line of bulletins and periodicals related to major occupational fields. The *BLS Update* is a quarterly newsletter available at your library (or by subscription) that lists the release dates of new or updated publications that can be ordered by mail. Most of these are either free of charge or reasonably priced, and are extremely valuable in the job-search effort. Similar data are also available on the BLS Data Diskette, which can be used with IBM-compatible personal computers or Lotus 1-2-3 (Version 1A or Version 2).

Some of the BLS publications I have found useful are:

> *Dictionary of Occupational Titles*
> *Exploring Careers*
> *Guide for Occupational Exploration*
> *Projection 2000*
> *Occupational Outlook Handbook*
> *Occupational Outlook Quarterly.*

The last two are my favorites. The *Handbook,* updated every two years, is a great place to start your career search, especially if you are uncertain about your chosen field. The *Quarterly,* available at the library or by subscription, complements the *Handbook* with articles about popular (and many times off-beat) careers.

For more information about BLS publications, write:

Bureau of Labor Statistics
441 G Street, N.W.
Washington, D.C. 20212

Business Organizations, Agencies, and Publications Directory (Gale Research Company). Republished every two years, this directory lists names, addresses, and points of contact of more than 2,400 organizations, along with related publications and other data sources regarding: trade, commercial, and labor organizations; government agencies and diplomatic offices; stock exchanges; the banking, tourism, and publishing industries; and computer information services.

Directory of Jobs and Careers Abroad (Vacation-Work, Oxford, England). Republished every three years (latest edition, 1992) this reference lists more than five hundred agencies, consultants, and associations, along with overseas branches, affiliates, and subsidiaries of British companies and other organizations that assist in locating permanent employment abroad. The worldwide coverage is arranged first by career fields, then geographically.

Directory of Leading Private Companies (Reed Publishing). This is a source of accurate information on private companies who do business in excess of ten million dollars. Key information includes addresses, telephone numbers, approximate annual earnings, number of employees, and names and titles of key officers. Once you have made some tentative career-field decisions, this is a great place to spot some of the emerging companies with a future.

A Final Word. These resources, though extremely useful, are but the tip of the iceberg. The real trick in staying on top of a constant flow of job-related information from many sources is to *get to know your librarians*. These creative and resourceful folks can save you hours of wheel spinning, by putting the right references for your career search into your hands. Just step up to the desk and ask.

ABOUT THE AUTHORS

FREDERICK A. MASTIN, JR., has served five years' active duty and fifteen years in the Selected Marine Corps Reserve. Working in the sales and marketing departments of *Fortune* 500 companies, he rose from trainee to national sales manager. He ran his own executive-recruiting program for seven years, and designed a career-transition program that has been used at military bases nationwide for the past ten years.

Involved in outplacement for all branches and all ranks of the armed services, Fred Mastin has conducted seminars and workshops nationwide, along with private counseling. The Navy, Marine Corps, and Veterans Administration have sought his counsel and advice. He has spoken before military, veterans, and civic organizations, has appeared on television and radio talk shows, and has seen his work published in military newspapers and professional journals.

Raised in Garden City, Long Island, he is a graduate of Siena College in New York, and currently resides in Branford, Connecticut.

JOHN GRIDER MILLER is a retired colonel of Marines and the managing editor of the Naval Institute *Proceedings*. An infantry officer with two combat tours in Vietnam, he also served as principal speechwriter for three commandants of the Marine Corps.

He is the author of *The Battle to Save the Houston* (1985) and *The Bridge at Dong Ha* (1989), for the Naval Institute Press.

Raised in the Washington, D.C., area, he is a graduate of Yale University and currently resides in Annapolis, Maryland.

INDEX

Accents, regional, 118–20
Accountability, 3, 32
Achievement and job interviews, 135f
Actuaries, career opportunities, as, 65–66
Administrative
  career opportunities, 62
  skills, 32
Affluence and success, 2
Aging population
  mature marketing, 68
  travel and tourism, 68–69
Agriculture career opportunities, 62
Akers, John, 55
Appearance, 3
  bearing and demeanor, 118
  body language, 120–21
  dress, 123–30
  grooming, 116–18, 129, 139
  language, use of, 118–20
  mannerisms, 120
  See also Manners; Wardrobe
Apple Computer, 40
Artistic occupations, 37
Attitude and employers, 21–22

Bearing and job interviews, 118
Benefits. *See* Salary and benefits

Benson, Herbert, 182
Biotechnology field, career
  opportunities in, 66
Bixler, Susan, 182
Body language and job interviews, 120–21
Bonuses, 173
Bureau of Labor Statistics
    Publications (BLS)
  BLS *Update*, 184
  Exploring Careers, 184
  Occupational Exploration, Guide
    for, 184
  Occupational Outlook
    Handbook, 184
  Occupational Outlook Quarterly,
    184
  Occupational Titles, Dictionary
    of, 184
  Projection 2000, 184
Bureaucracy, understanding, 33
Business ethics, 55–61
Business trends
*Business Organizations, Agencies,
    and Publications Directory*,
    184–85
  Cold War, end of, 54–55
  corporate downsizing, 54, 56
  deregulation, 54

tax reform, 54
Business world, 53–61
  ethical codes, 58–59
  fraud, waste, and abuse, 54, 56–61
  job related stress, 57–58

Calling. *See* Vocation
Camp Lejeune seminar, 6–7
Career
  finding, 61–73
  and regrouping, 25–26, 27
  and retirement, 20, 22
Career choices, 35–43
  dreams, 41–43
  interests, 35–39
  needs, 39–41
  See also Priorities; Strong-
    Campbell Interest Inventory
Career opportunities, 61–73
  administrative, 62
  administrative support, 62
  agriculture, 62
  construction, 62
  executive, 62
  fishing, 62
  forestry, 62
  installers, 62
  managerial, 62
  marketing and sales, 62
  mechanics, 62
  production, 62
  professional specialty, 62
  repairers, 62
  service, 62
  technicians, 62
  transportation, 62
  See also Aging population;
    Ecology; Health fields;
    Overseas
Career search. *See* Employment,
  routes to; Interviews; Job
  search; Résumés

Center for Decision Research, 44
Chamber of Commerce, 99
Civic organizations and job
  opportunities, 105
CivLand, definition of, 20n
Cold War, end of, 54–55
Color for Men (Jackson), 182
Color Me Beautiful (Jackson), 182
Commissions, 173
Communication and job interviews,
  135f, 136–37
Company travel, 173
Compensation, as career priority,
  47, 48–50, 51f
Competitive spirit and job
  interviews, 135f
Conflict resolution and job
  interviews, 135f
Construction trades, career
  opportunities in, 62, 67
Conventional occupations, 38
Conventions and job opportunities,
  104–5
Cover letter
  body, 86–87
  checking, 88
  closing, 87–88
  heading, 86
  salutation, 86
  sample, 90f
  See also Interviews; Third Party
    Letters; Résumés
Creative marking, 110–11
Creativity, 3, 33
  as a need, 41
  and the job search, 96

Dale Carnegie public-speaking
  courses, 107
Decision making, 3, 33
Decision research, 44–45
Dedication, 3, 33
Defense-related employment,

reduction of, 56–57
Demeanor and job interviews, 118
Demilitarizing résumés, 83–84
Deming, Dr. W. Edwards, 57
Derek, Bo, 115
Design field, career opportunities in, 67
Detail, attention to, 3, 33
Disability, 173
Domino's pizza, 40
Dressing. *See* Wardrobe

EAS Work-Sheet, 29f, 31
Ecology
    environmental engineer, 68
Education, 3, 33
    and job interviews, 135f
    and success, 2
Employers, 20–22
    and attitude, 21–22
    and personal qualities, 21
Employment, routes to, 98–113
    advertising yourself, 108
    agencies, 99
    Chamber of Commerce, 99, 106
    civic organizations, 105
    contact lists, 103–4
    contacts, 102–3
    conventions, 104–5
    detail, attention to, 109
    executive search firms, 99
    industry trade shows, 104–5
    libraries, 100–1
    military associations, 100
    networking, 101–2, 109
    newspapers, 98–99
    nontraditional, 109–12
    outplacement services, 99
    related careers, 109
    resource directory, 101
    right approach, 112–13
    speechmaking, 106–7
    state employment commission, 99

trade shows, 104–5
    volunteering, 107–8
    working without pay, 105–6
    See also Job search; Résumés
Employment Agencies, 99
Encyclopedia of Associations, 64, 69, 183
Energy and job interviews, 135f
Enterprising occupations, 37–38, 46
Esprit de corps, 40
Ethics and business, 56–61
Ethics Resource Center, 58
Ethnic heritage and success, 2
Executive career opportunities, 62
Executive search firms, 99
Exploring Careers (BLS), 184
Eye contact and job interview, 139, 140–41

Family
    as career priority, 47–48, 48–50, 52f
    and regrouping, 22–23, 27
Federal service, 182–83
Finances and regrouping, 24, 27
Fishing industry career opportunities, 62
Flexibility and job interviews, 135f
Ford, Henry, 33
Forehandedness, 3, 32–33
Forestry industry career opportunities, 62
Friends and regrouping, 23, 27
Functional skills, 31

Gabor, Zsa Zsa,
Grooming and job interviews, 116–18, 129, 139
Group interviews, 132, 134–135

Hair. *See* Grooming for interviews
Handshakes, 122

at interview, 139–40
Health and regrouping, 23–24, 27
Health-maintenance field, career
    opportunities in, 65
Health fields
    actuaries, 65–66
    assistants, 67
    biotechnology, 66
    design and construction, 67
    health-maintenance, 65
    home health care, 67
    special-education teacher, 67–68
    technologists, 67
    therapists, 67
Heilig, Gabe, 183
Hewlett-Packard, 40
High-tech, familiarity with, 33
Home health care, career
    opportunities in, 67
Honesty, 3, 32
Humor, sense of
    and the job search, 97

Iacocca, Lee, 169
Imagination and job interviews,
    135f
Individuality as a need, 41
Industry trade shows and job
    opportunities, 104–5
Initiative and job interviews, 135f
Innovation, 3, 33
Installers, career opportunities as,
    62
Integrity, 3, 32
Intelligence and job interviews,
    135f
International Business Machines
    (IBM), 55–56
Interviewers' criteria, 135
    achievement, 135f
    communication, 135f, 136–37
    competitive spirit, 135f
    conflict resolution, 135f

education and skills, 135f
energy, 135f
flexibility, 135f
imagination, 135f
initiative, 135f
intelligence, 135f
leadership, 135f
responsibility, 135f
self-confidence, 135f
self-knowledge, 134f
sense of purpose, 134f
Interviews, 131–55
    first impression, 137–38, 139–41
    group, 132, 134–35
    questions, 141–55
    screening, 132, 133
    serial, 132
    stress, 133
    See also Cover letter; Job offer;
        Résumés
Interviews, mistakes, 138–39
    being late, 139
    eye contact, 139, 140–41
    derogatory remarks, 139
    dressing inappropriately, 139
    handshake, 139, 139–40
    knowledge of company, 139
    rambling answers, 139
    salary and benefits, 139
    self-assessment, 139
    smoking and gum, 139
Interviews, preparing for, 114–30
    bearing and demeanor, 118
    body language, 120–21
    grooming, 116–18, 129, 139
    language, use of, 118–20
    mannerisms, 120
    See also Manners; Wardrobe
Inventory process, 27–34
    accomplishments, 30–31
    action verbs, 31f
    EAS Work-Sheet, 29f, 31
    experience, 28–30

skills, 30–32
Investigative occupations, 37

Jackson, Carole, 125, 182
Job offer, 156–78
    company, criticism of, 161–62
    notes, reviewing, 161
    questions, 156–60
    rejection, 164–66
    staying alert, 161
Job related stress, 57–58
Job search, 96–98
    creativity and, 96
    perseverance and, 96
    records, importance of keeping,
        97–98
    and a sense of humor, 97
    See also Employment, routes to;
        Résumés
*Jobs and Careers Abroad,
    Directory of*, 85

Language and job interviews, 118–
    20
Leadership and job interviews,
    135f
*Leading Private Companies,
    Directory of*, 185
Librarians and job information, 185
Life-style, as career priority, 47–
    48, 48–50, 52f
List making, 9, 12
Loyalty, 3, 33

Management-incentive plans, 174
Managerial
    career opportunities, 62
    skills, 32
Mannerisms, 120
Manners, 121–23
    elevators, leaving, 122
    first names, using, 122
    grabbing the check, 122

making conversation, 122–23
saying goodby, 123
shaking hands, 122
taking seats, 122
Marine Corps
    military associations, 100
    outplacement services, 99
    promotion system, 7, 11
Marine Corps Council, 100
Marine Executive Association, 100
Marketing career opportunities, 62
Mechanics, career opportunities as,
    62
Medical benefits, 172–73
Military associations, 100
Mindset, establishing, 22–26
Motivational leadership, 3, 33–34

National Business Employment,
    100
Needs, deeply felt
    creativity, 41
    esprit de corps, 40
    individuality, 41
    product, belief in, 40–41
Networking, 101–2, 109
New York Times
    on success, 2
Non-Commissioned Officers
    Association (NCOA), 100,
    181
Northwestern National Life
    job related stress, study on, 57–
    58

*Occupational Exploration, Guide
    for* (BLS), 184
Occupational Outlook Handbook
    (BLS), 62–64, 184
Occupational Outlook Quarterly
    (BLS), 63, 184
Occupational Titles, Dictionary of
    (BLS), 184

Occupations. *See* Career
  opportunities
Outplacement services, 99
Overseas
  accountant, 69
  entrepreneur, 69
Overtime, 174

Paid vacations, 174
Perseverance, 3, 33
  and the job search, 96
Personal qualities and employers,
  21
Personal traits
  bureaucracy, understanding of,
    33
  decision making, 3, 33
  dedication and loyalty, 3, 33
  education and training, 3, 33
  forehandedness, 3, 32–33
  high-tech familiarity, 33
  honesty and integrity, 3, 32
  innovation and creativity, 3, 33
  motivational leadership, 3, 33–
    34
  physical fitness and appearance,
    3
  practicality and attention to
    detail, 3, 33
  responsibility and accountability,
    3, 32
  self-discipline, 3, 32
  steadiness and perseverance, 3,
    33
  work ethic, 3, 32
Physical fitness, 3
Poverty and success, 2
Practicality, 3, 33
Priorities, 43–50, 51–52f
  calling and career, 46–47, 48–
    50, 51f
  compensation, 47, 48–50, 51f
  deciding, 43–48

family and life-style, 47–48, 48–
    50, 52f
  setting, 48–50
  See also Career choices
Product
  belief in, 40–41
  quality, 56–61
Production, career opportunities in,
  62
Professional conferences and job
  opportunities, 104–5
Professional Image, The (Bixler),
  182
Professional specialty career
  opportunities, 62
Projection 2000 (BLS), 184
Purpose, sense of, 134f

Quality. *See under* Product
Quality technology. *See* Total
  Quality Leadership

Radner, Gilda, 116
Realistic occupations, 37
Rejection, 164–66
Relaxation Response, The
  (Benson), 182
Relocation, 174
Repairers, career opportunities as,
  62
Resource directory, 101, 181–85
  business directories, 184–85
  federal service, 182–83
  general references, 183–84
  image, color, and style, 182
  interests, determining, 181–82
  stress management, 182
Responsibility, 3, 32
  and job interviews, 135f
Résumés, 74–95
  age, 82–83
  creative packaging, 84–85
  demilitarize, 83–84

drafts as a ploy, 84
mobility, 83
objective, 82
See also Cover letter;
  Employment, routes to;
  Interviews; Job search
Résumés, chronological, 77–78
  sample, 91–92f
Résumés, functional, 77, 78–79
  sample, 93–94f
Résumés, targeted, 77, 79–81
  accomplishments, 79, 80–81
  capabilities, 79, 80
  job target, 79, 80
  miscellaneous, 79–80
  sample, 95f
  work history and education, 81
Résumés, traps to avoid
  bizarre packaging, 76–77, 84–85
  distortions, 76
  grammatical errors, 76
  graphic appeal, lack of, 75
  information, lack of, 76
  irrelevant material, 76
  overwritten, 76
  poor reproduction, 75
  spelling errors, 76
  typographical errors, 76
Retired Officers Association, The
  (TROA), 100, 181
Retirement
  dreams of, 41–43
  qualifying for, 182–83
  and a second career, 20, 22
Retirement plans, 174
Regional patterns and success, 2
Regrouping. *See* Wheel, spokes of
Rickover, Hyman, 133

Salary and benefits
  accepting, 178
  bonuses and commissions, 173
  company travel, 173

disability and sick leave, 173
  inappropriate questions, 139
  management-incentive plans, 174
  medical benefits, 172–73
  moving, 174
  negotiating, 166–70, 175–78
  the offer, 170–72
  overtime, 174
  paid vacation, 174
  retirement plan, 174
  training and education, 173–74
Sales, career opportunities in, 62
SCII occupational themes
  artistic, 37
  conventional, 38
  enterprising, 37–38, 46
  investigative, 37
  realistic, 37
  social, 37, 46
Screening interviews, 132, 133
Self-confidence and job interviews,
  135f
Self-discipline, 3, 32
Self-inventory, 26–34
  documents, organization of, 26–
    28
  shortcuts, 26–27
  See also Inventory process;
    Wheel, spokes of
Self-knowledge, 134f
Selye, Hans, 182
Serial interviews, 132
Service industry career
  opportunities, 62
Sick leave, 173
Skills
  administrative, 32
  functional, 31
  and job interviews, 135f
  managerial, 32
  technical, 32
Social occupations, 37, 46
Special-education teacher, career

opportunities as, 67–68
Spirituality and regrouping, 24–25, 27
State employment commission, 99
Steadiness, 3, 33
Stevenson, Adlai, 128
Stress
  interviews, 133
  management, 182
Stress Without Distress (Selye), 182
Strong-Campbell Interest Inventory (SCII), 37–38, 181–82. *See also* SCII occupational themes
Success
  and affluence, 2
  and education, 2
  and ethnic heritage, 2
  and poverty, 2
  and regional patterns, 2
Success, components of, 2–4. *See also* Personal traits

Technical skills, 32
Technicians, career opportunities as, 62
Technologists, career opportunities as, 67
Therapists, career opportunities as, 67
Third Party Letters, 88
  See also Résumés
Toastmaster clubs, 107
Total Quality Leadership, 57–61
Toys-for-Tots, 106–7
Training, 3, 33
Transportation industry career opportunities, 62

Vocation
  as career priority, 46–47, 48–50, 51f
Volunteering, 107–8

Wardrobe
  the basics, 124–26
  buttondown collars, 127
  choosing, 123–24
  cuffs, 126
  dark suits, 126
  glasses, 128
  inappropriate, 139
  jewelry, 128
  neck size and sleeve length, 127
  pens and pencils, 128
  pinstripes, 126
  and quality, 126
  shirts, cotton, 127
  shirts, polyester, 127
  shoes, 127–28
  socks, 128
  ties, 127
  ties, knots, 127
  ties, power, 127
  two-button suits, 126
  vests, 126
  white shirts, 127
Wardrobe, women
  accessories, 129
  blazer vs. suit, 129
  classic style, 128
  coordinating, 128–29
  fragrance, 129
  grooming, 129
  pantyhose, 129
  shoes, 129
Wharton Business School
  MBA program, 59–60
Wheel, spokes of
  career, 25–26, 27
  family, 22–23, 27
  finances, 24, 27
  friends, 23, 27
  health, 23–24, 27
  spirituality, 24–25, 27
Winters, Robyn, 128, 182
Work ethic, 3, 32